NINETY SECONDS
TO MIDNIGHT

HOW – EUGENICS – PANDEMICS – GLOBAL GOVERNMENT
PLANET X AND APOPHIS ARE ABOUT TO DESTROY OUR WORLD

CHRISTOPHER WHITE

Grosvenor House
Publishing Limited

This book is published by
Grosvenor House Publishing Ltd
Link House
140 The Broadway, Tolworth, Surrey, KT6 7HT.
www.grosvenorhousepublishing.co.uk

A CIP record for this book
is available from the British Library

ISBN 978-1-80381-511-4

'For we do not wrestle against flesh and blood, but against the rulers, against the authorities, against the cosmic powers, over this present darkness, against the spiritual forces of evil in the heavenly places.' Ephesians 6:12. *English Standard Version*

Acknowledgements

With thanks to Dr Mike Lockwood, Adam Houghton' Ian Long and Andy Lee for their support, advice and practical assistance in putting this book together and my wife Sandra for her valuable insights.

Contents

Foreword

In 1947, the Chicago Atomic Scientists, who had worked on the Manhattan project and created the first nuclear bomb, produced a measurement on how close they believed mankind was towards nuclear annihilation. They called this measurement 'The Doomsday Clock'. This clock is now reset each year by The Science and Security Board Bulletin of Atomic Scientists. In 1947, the clock was first set at 7 minutes to midnight and over the years has been pushed forwards or backwards depending on the perceived level of threat facing humanity.

On 23rd of January 2023, the clock, which now includes analysis on additional threats caused by climate change, biological dangers and disruptive technologies was set at 90 seconds to midnight and determines that mankind again faces 'a time of unprecedented danger.' However, one area that has been omitted from this analysis is the growing number of threats coming from space. NASA are now so concerned about this they have run a series of preparation exercises and published reports on the levels of disruption that would be caused by an asteroid strike.

In a democracy there is an unspoken understanding of the civil liberties a government should afford its citizens. Sometimes, like the United States, a written constitution or agreement is in place that provides for and protects all American's basic human rights. Our leaders promise to keep us safe from those who would do us harm, ensure that we live in a relatively clean environment, drink clean water, are allowed to own property and live a life without undue Government interference or coercion. We make use of Government provided schools, colleges, universities and libraries to further our prospects, and in the UK, make use of a National Health Service that provides care at the point of need. We are also allowed to go where we wish, meet with whoever we want (within reason) and live a meaningful, productive life.

As our part of this covenant, we are expected to act as good citizens, obey the law, pay our taxes and work hard to develop a lifestyle that best befits our social status. To reward our efforts over a long career we receive a pension so that we can have a reasonable standard of living in our senior years.

Sadly, this covenant has been irrevocably broken by our Governments due to discoveries in space in the 1970's and 1980's that will soon bring about a series of near extinction events and the establishment of a One World Government. This book will reveal what these events are and how our leaders are implementing a plan to prepare us psychologically for what's approaching.

Because law and order is shortly expected to break down, control is quickly being transferred to an elite shadow world government-in-waiting, who have recruited a network of globalist billionaires to use their exponential wealth to develop alternative power structures. Their intentions are to wrest power away from our democratically elected Governments. That is why it makes very little difference who you vote for, as the script has been written already. Today's real power brokers who transcend elected governments are a network of 'Illuminated' Masonic Lodges and organisations like the Bilderberg Group, The World Economic Forum, The World Health Organisation and the United Nations.

However a number of politicians, pastors, medical professionals, scientists and 'influencers' are now speaking out, creating awareness and taking action to prevent a further erosion of our civil liberties. The Bible informs us that just before Christ's return, the Earth will undergo a number of significant changes and that man will turn away from his Creator and become completely deluded. The Globalists are now using wars, disasters, plagues and pandemics to bring about the establishment of a New World Order, just as they are currently using our fears and insecurities to mandate their vaccine protocols.

The factors that create an opportunity for the corporate banking dynasties to quickly transform a democracy into a dictatorship, nearly always involve political upheaval and a financial meltdown. The rise of the Nazi Party is a prime example of this. The current orchestrated financial crisis will lead this generation into a cashless society based on Central Bank Digital Currencies that can only be accessed by a biologically placed microchip. This has already been planned and patented by Bill Gates. We are beginning to see the formation of another totalitarian regime targeting individuals who refuse to get the Covid vaccine as 'conspiracy theorists.' Substances that the pharmaceutical companies have placed within their vaccines and are concealing from the population will be revealed.

The experimental nature of the Moderna, AstraZeneca, Johnson & Johnson and Pfizer vaccines means that those who have suffered vaccine injuries are unable to claim compensation. The television, radio and newspapers controlled by the Globalists, are silent on this matter and are refusing to inform the public about the issues being experienced by millions of people, who believed that their lives would get better and we would return to normal after inoculation.

The sources used for this book are peer-reviewed studies, United States Patents (which can't be denigrated as fake news) NASA documentation, personal testimonies and historical news articles that can still be accessed by the general public. I examine biblical prophecy relating to a time period known as the Great Tribulation, mainly using the New Revised Standard Version, (unless stated). I also use Apocryphal literature and the book of Enoch, which was specifically written for the Tribulation saints.

Chapter 1

The Nazis in America –
A Warning from History

Perhaps you are familiar with the story of the 'Monuments Men'[1] who sought out stolen gold, priceless pictures and artefacts that the Nazis had pillaged from European museums. By January 1945, the war was nearly over and the Luftwaffe had lost control of the skies. This provided an opportunity for the Joint Intelligence Objectives Agency, a hastily amalgamated group, to locate and detain the German scientists who had helped the Nazis to develop their vast array of wonder-weapons, (Wunderwaffe's) and take them to America before they fell into Soviet hands.

One of Hitler's wonder-weapons was an organophosphate called Tabun[3]. On April 16th 1945, in a heavily forested area seventy-five miles west of Hanover, British soldiers from Montgomery's Twenty First Army Group discovered two large caches of bombs in an abandoned testing area that was known locally as the Robber's Lair or Raubkammer. The first pile of bombs was quickly identified as mustard gas, but the second pile marked with three green lines contained a substance the Military were unfamiliar with. After some delay to allow chemists to examine the find, and by making local enquiries, the bombs were found to contain Tabun. When it was tested on animals, they found a small drop placed on the skin could kill in a matter of seconds, causing the glands and muscles to over-stimulate and the respiratory system to fail. This substance was one of the deadliest known to man and if dropped from German bombers it could have obliterated the Red Army, but was never used in the field of conflict. We can only speculate that Hitler, having been bombed with mustard gas in the World War One trenches could not conceive of using this highly effective but diabolical weapon.

Military Intelligence finally convinced Harry Truman to bring Nazi scientists into America. Those considered suitable for transfer had a paperclip placed on their file and 'Operation Paperclip' was born. As the President had agreed that only those 'on the 'periphery' of the Nazi Party would be considered, subterfuge was used to whitewash the history of depraved Nazi murderers and re-invent them as 'good Nazis', as long as they had something to offer the growing US Military complex. Starting from 1945, and continuing to 1959, over 1600[4] Nazis scientists who were expert in the fields of chemical development and aeronautics, escaped justice at Nuremburg. They were reprieved then shipped over to the United States. This would effectively assist the US to gain military and scientific superiority over the Communists and eventually place a man on the moon.

After the war ended, experiments with Tabun were conducted by the military and the newly formed Central Intelligence Agency at the Dugway Proving Ground in Utah. In 1947 a synthetically reduced version of Tabun was fed into gassing chambers to a group of army 'volunteers.' The tests were conducted by Dr. L Wilson Greene who noticed that, although the volunteers were partially disabled, disorientated and badly affected by fatigue, sometimes for months, they all eventually recovered. Dr. Greene realised that this new form of 'psycho-chemical' warfare would be of great value, as it was not only 'non-lethal,' it would also dramatically reduce an army's ability to wage war while keeping the country's infrastructure intact.

Those who found themselves heading to America under 'Paperclip' are as follows:[7] Otto Ambros had developed Sarin Gas for the Nazis and was known as Hitler's Chemist. Found guilty at the Nuremberg Trials of mass murder and slavery, Ambros was granted clemency by the High Commissioner. Friedrich Hoffman was another chemist who was also exonerated and later worked for the Central Intelligence Agency, synthesising Nazi nerve gas and worked in their assassination-by-poison programme; Walter Dornberger was in charge of V Weapon development for the Reich. Charged with war crimes and described as 'a menace of the first order'. Dornberger was eventually released into US Custody; Dr Siegfried Ruff was Director of the German Experimental Station for Aviation Medicine. Ruff supervised medical murder experiments. He was tried at Nuremberg and acquitted; Walter Riedal, engineer for the V Weapons programme, threatened to work for the Russians if they did not take him to the US under Paperclip.

Others involved in V Weapon development and released under Paperclip were: Arthur Rudolph, in charge of a slave labour facility in Nordhausen; Georg Rickhey, General Manager of the V2 Rocket programme and slave labour facility at Nordhausen; Kurt Debus, another V Weapons engineer was described as an 'ardent Nazi' but eventually worked with Werner von Brown to become the first Director of NASA's John F Kennedy's Space Centre in Florida.

After the war, Klaus Barbie, the 'Butcher of Lyon', who had managed to escape the Allies dragnet, was recruited by American Intelligence and stayed in Germany reporting on Communist activities in Eastern Europe. He was protected by the Americans until 1951 when French pressure to arrest him became unsustainable. The US Intelligence Service eventually provided Barbie with a false passport and supporting documentation under the name of Klaus Altmann. Barbie finally fled from Germany with his family after receiving a $5000 gift to thank him for his services to the American Government and was given safe passage to South America.

How Nazis possessed so many technically advanced weapons may indicate that their primary origins and inspiration were not human at all, but from the dark spirit realm.[9] The leaders of the Third Reich were completely steeped in occult and Black Magic practices. During the time that the Nazis were in ascendency, a group of female mediums, called 'The Vril,' began channelling messages from supposed 'extra-terrestrials' on how to develop their wonder-weapons. Vril women wore their hair long as they believed it acted as 'cosmic antenna' to assist them to receive messages in automatic hand-writing. The Vril were from the inner circle of the Thule Society which exuded huge influence over the Nazi leadership from 1922-1945.

At a meeting in an old hunting lodge at Berchtesgaden in 1919, Maria Orsic[10] presented to representatives of the Thule, Vril and Black Sun societies, telepathic messages she claimed she had received from a civilisation located sixty-eight light years away in the constellation of Taurus. When the message was translated it was found to be in a secret Germanic Templer code and provided plans for the development of a spherical shaped flying ship that closely resembles the shape of today's UFO sightings. The Vril described their telepathic contacts as 'Nordic' looking and about 6 foot to 6 foot 6 inches tall. Hitler claims to have seen one of these visitors and that he was 'evil beyond belief.' The irony of that statement was obviously lost on him!

It was two years after the war ended, that the United States Government formed the Central Intelligence Agency. This became the dumping ground for a number of high ranking Nazi protagonists who assisted the CIA to develop and improve their interrogation techniques. Not only had the Allies de-nazification programme been an abject failure, but by the beginning of the 1950's, the CIA had itself become completely saturated in Nazi ideology, developing their own torture, terror and mind control experiments. In 1951 the CIA started its 'Artichoke' Programme.[11] This placed two unwitting young girls into a deep hypnotic state. Using a number of coded words, one of the girls successfully completed the test of constructing and planting a fake incendiary device and took it to a chosen designation.

Drawing on the positive outcomes of Artichoke; in 1953 MKULTRA[12] was authorised by the then Director of Central Intelligence, Mr Allen W Dulles. The programme lasted for 10 years. MKULTRA used more comprehensive mind control techniques including sleep deprivation, torture, sexual abuse and feeding their victims on a cocktail of illicit drugs, mainly LSD, to expand the human conscience and develop each subject's telekinetic potential. Forced subjugation was not only against the Nuremberg Code, but the CIA went even further to protect all those who were involved in this de-humanising treatment, by intentionally shredding all the files relating to the project. The Investigations Committee had to rely on personal testimony alone from the victims of ULTRA.

The Nazi War Crimes and Japanese Imperial Records Interagency Working Group were founded on January 11th 1999. One of the IWG's tasks was to investigate the cosy relationship that had developed between former post war Nazi war criminals and the CIA. Although the damning documentation was initially withheld, thousands of pages of evidence were eventually unearthed by the IWG. In 2002, they were able to de-classify 97 key documents from SECRET RELGER and eight million other documents from multiple Government Agencies.[13] These provided highly detailed accounts of the close working relationship between US Government departments, the CIA and known Nazi war criminals. While Nazi hunters like Simon Wiesenthal were attempting to capture high ranking Nazis like Adolph Eichmann, the CIA had searched out and recruited five of Eichmann's 'associates' for their own subversive work. This included Alto Von Bolschwing who worked closely with Eichmann and made it his mission to 'purge Germany of all the Jews.'

Former Congresswoman, Elizabeth Holtman, a public member of the IWG stated, 'I think that the CIA has defied the law and in so doing has also trivialised the Holocaust, thumbed its nose at the survivors of the Holocaust and also the Americans who gave their lives in the effort to defeat the Nazis in World War Two.'

Chapter 2

Simon Wiesenthal–Nazi Hunter

In the spring of 1946, Nazi hunter, Simon Wiesenthal, was sifting through some paperwork when he found some information that he described as 'one of the most amazing documents to have fallen into Allied hands since the end of the war.' Knowing that Wiesenthal was building dossiers on Nazi war criminals, an American officer casually brought a rucksack into Wiesenthal's Office in Linz.[14] It contained a large dark blue file that the officer had taken from Oberst Keitel, who worked at the Ebensee S.S. Internment Camp near Bad Ischl. The file contained the minutes of a top secret meeting of leading German Industrialists in Strasbourg.

On 10th August 1944, at the hotel Maison Rouge in Strasbourg and without the knowledge of the S.S, the Schutzstaffel[14] (Hitler's executive bodyguard unit), a clandestine gathering took place of leading German Industrialists who were adjusting to the realisation that Hitler would probably lose the war, and arrangements would have to be made to safeguard Nazi treasures from the Allies.

A technical network would have to be set up all over the world that would be able to co-ordinate future efforts. Among those present at Maison Rouge were representatives from Rochling Concern, Krupp, Messerschmidt, the Goring-Werke in Linz, and top officials from the War and Armaments Ministries. The Chairman, Dr Scheid, made this telling statement. 'Germany has already lost the battle of France. From now on Germany's industry must prepare for the economic post-war campaign. Every industrialist must seek contact with firms abroad, each for himself, without drawing attention and that is not all! *We must be ready to finance the Nazi Party, which will be forced to go underground for some time.'* (Italics mine)

A report issued by the US Treasury Department in 1946, found that Nazi Industrialists had purchased 750 Companies.[15] 214 were set up in Switzerland, 112 in Spain, 98 in Argentina, 58 in Portugal, 35 in Turkey and a further 233 in various other countries. This would provide a sizeable war chest for the furtherance of a future Fourth Reich's aims and objectives in post war Europe, while using its wealth to control and influence major corporations.

At the same time, the ODESSA network[16] was formed and the underground organisation of SS Officers provided a series of bolt holes for prominent Nazis fleeing the Allies, and dropping off points for their looted treasures. German officers suddenly found that second accounts had been opened up in their names that they knew nothing about, containing millions of Marks. Hospitals that had been set up, to supposedly treat wounded SS officers, were, in fact, dropping off points for Nazi bullion, which was being transported via ambulances that were marked with the Red Cross logo.[17] One seized delivery note of assets being sent from Berlin to Altaussee, an area that had mysteriously grown in population in one year from 18,000 to 80,000, contained the following;

50 kilograms of gold bars
50 cases of gold coins and gold articles, each case weighing 100 pounds
2 million American dollars and 2 million Swiss franks
5 cases filled with diamonds and precious stones
1 stamp collection worth at least 5 million gold Marks

In some instances, gold[18] was concealed in the roofs of houses as camouflaged gold bricks. One of the houses was so overloaded with gold that the roof collapsed and the gold was requisitioned by the French authorities. Through their efforts near the end of the war, Nazis had secured assets worth staggering amounts of money and provided safe refuge for thousands of individuals wanted for war crimes. With the extra benefit of 'Operation Paperclip,' plus the 750 companies started up with looted gold, the Nazis were in a strong position to maintain their field of influence abroad and further the aims of a future Fourth Reich for the rich, or as Klaus Schwab from the World Economic Forum now coins it, 'The Fourth Industrial Revolution.'

No lessons have been learned from past Nazi atrocities as we find ourselves sliding towards another attempt at world dictatorship. This time the Globalists are using the current pandemic and 'climate emergency' as a tool to control our lives. This euphemistically called 'Fourth Industrial Revolution' is in truth a pro Communist cashless society where a few rule the roost, private ownership is abolished and we all work for a pittance as long as we respond correctly to the obedience tools *they* will put in place. The New World Order conspirators are a new breed of technocrats, bankers, global businessmen and drug barons who want to inoculate people they consider 'eugenically inferior' with dangerous substances, and give us all a bar code turning us into worker drones. These are the new 'untouchables', who readily circumvent laws and Government restrictions for their own advantage.

Chapter 3

America's and Germany's Eugenics Programme

Sir Francis Galton was a biological determinist and cousin of Charles Darwin and who first used the word[19] 'Eugenics' to describe the 'Race Theory' he developed in the 1880's. Although he was the inventor of the fingerprint identification system, he had concluded that certain people groups were inferior to others and needed to be controlled through 'selective breeding.' Galton wrote a number of papers on the subject and was knighted in 1909.

The State of Connecticut[20] was the first to implement Galton's theories when in 1896 they prevented the marriage of individuals who had epilepsy or those the State Governors considered imbecilic or 'feeble minded.' By the end of the 1920's, with the imposition of racially based immigration controls, the use of compulsory sterilisation and the widespread ban on inter-racial marriage this gave American eugenicists the right to boast that they had made their nation the 'most eugenically pure state in the world.'[21]

The Eugenics Board of North Carolina formed in 1933[22] by State Legislature, enacted an amendment to Chapter 34 of the public laws of 1929 regarding the sterilisation of persons they considered mentally defective or feeble minded. Of the 7,687 people who were coerced into being sterilised in North Carolina after 1933, 5000 were black. The board was only officially wound down and closed by Legislature in 1977. In the case of

'Buck vs Bell,'[23] held at the US Supreme Court, Oliver Wendell Holmes Jr. ruled that a state statute permitting compulsory sterilisation of the 'unfit' including the 'intellectually disabled 'did not violate the 'due process' clause of the 14th amendment of the US. This is now considered one of the worst Supreme Court decisions ever made. On May 2nd 1927 in an 8-1 majority verdict, the US Supreme Court ordered that Carrie Buck, whom it called 'a feeble minded daughter of a feeble minded mother with a feeble minded child' be sterilised under the provision of the 1924 'Virginia Eugenically Sterilisation Act'.

So was it true that someone who was considered by the State to be imbecilic or feeble minded as introduced by Justice Wendell Holmes Jr, was fated to give birth to a generation of dysfunctional adults?[24] In 1979, the director of the hospital where Carrie Buck was sterilised, sought her out. It was found that neither Carrie Buck or her sister or her sister's daughter showed any signs of being 'feeble minded.' Carrie, had in fact, given birth to a child of normal intelligence. Like her sister, her only 'crime' was that she was born poor and powerless.

However, sterilisation was not the only method being thought up by the rich and powerful to eradicate the genes of those they considered morally and intellectually defective. Way back in 1911,[25] a report instigated by the Carnegie Institute explored eighteen methods of eradicating defective genetic attributes from society. The eighth method was euthanasia with the proviso of setting up a number of gas chambers throughout the US. However, the geneticists knew that the American public would find this abhorrent so decided to continue their murderous campaign in secret. In Lincoln Illinois,[26] mental institutions put their 'Social Darwinism' theories to the test when they gave their incoming patients milk, laced with tuberculosis, which lead to the deaths of over 40% of their residents. Only the very strong survived.

The Rockefeller Foundation's eugenics programme of the 1920's was also calling for the mass sterilisation and elimination of minority populations in America. In 1929 Rockefeller's chief executive, in charge of their eugenics institute, was the fascist Swiss psychiatrist[27] Ernst Rudin, assisted by his protégés Otmar Verschuer and Franz Kallmann. Josef Mengele was also working under the instructions of Verschuer and Kallmann who later went on to create the American Society of Human Genetics. This 'Society' became the precursor of the $3 billion Human Genome Project.

After the eugenics movement became well established in America, it extended its sphere of influence abroad with Californian eugenicists publishing literature for overseas consumption. In Germany, scientists were encouraged to sterilise those who were deemed to be defective. The Rockefeller foundation provided funding for a number of overseas programmes. Upon returning from Germany in 1934, where more than 5,000 people per month were being forcibly sterilized,[28] the Californian eugenics leader, C. M. Goethe, bragged to a colleague:

'You will be interested to know that your work has played a powerful part in shaping the opinions of the group of intellectuals who are behind Hitler in this epoch-making program. Everywhere, I sensed that their opinions have been tremendously stimulated by American thought... I want you, my dear friend, to carry this thought with you for the rest of your life, that you have really jolted into action a great government of 60 million people.'

Just as the Nazis were at the forefront of the eugenics movement in Europe, attempting to eradicate those who did not fit into their 'Master Race' theory, current attempts to manipulate and eradicate our own God given genetic code, is at the forefront of the New World Order's Satanically inspired plan for the complete enslavement of mankind, from the cradle to the grave.

Chapter 4

Obedience to Tyranny and Social Control

'It is always a simple matter to drag the people along whether it is a democracy, a Fascist dictatorship, a Parliament or a Communist dictatorship. Voice or no voice, the people can always be brought along to the bidding of the leaders. That is easy. All you have to tell them is they are being attacked, and denounce the pacifists for lack of patriotism, and exposing the country to greater danger. It works the same in any country.' Hermann Goring, at the Nuremburg war trials.

In the 1990's as part of my business degree, I was sent on a field trip with other students who visited a Japanese factory in Telford that were using 'Just In Time' (JIT) work practices. The factory itself resembled a small aircraft hangar. On the ground was a series of tram lines on which small robotic component carriers scurried their way to the workforce stopping only when it reached a pre-programmed crossroads where one robot would give way to another.

The component robot stopped between two workers, usually women, on an assembly line. In front of the women were compartmentalised trays with a picture of the diodes, capacitors and motherboards that workers would have to quickly place on the tray. The pre-assembled kit was then put onto a slow moving rubberised track, which delivered the goods to the team leader at the end of the line, who did a quick quality check and then sent them via another robot to the installation crew. If any of the workers needed a toilet break, they had to press a button, which would light up a panel above their heads. The team leader would then take their place until they returned.

Weekly progress sheets were placed on a notice board where teams could compare their performance with other teams. One aspect of the Japanese work practices that did not have the desired results was the use of company 'Shame Boards' where a team or individual would have a written message about their poor performance placed above their heads. Rather than bringing embarrassment, the boards were a constant source of amusement. As they were not improving production, the company decided to remove them. I was surprised just how quickly the Unions were willing to adapt their workforce to controlling and quite demeaning work practises introduced by the Japanese, which they would have previously frowned upon.

To question or oppose our managers in the industrial, political or scientific arenas, takes a huge amount of moral courage, and whistleblowers are sometimes vilified by those closest to them. Much better then to keep your head down and take the road of least resistance than the road less travelled and get your head blown off!

In 1960, Adolph Eichmann was arrested and subsequently stood trial in Jerusalem for crimes against humanity, on 11th April 1961.[29] However, the prosecution made a serious error in trying to portray Eichmann as a monster. Rather than looking like the crucible of evil that everyone expected, Eichmann's physical appearance with his thinning grey hair and gaunt features made him appear more like a nondescript librarian than a mass murderer - the sort of man that people would casually pass in the street without a second glance. How could such an ordinary man perpetuate such atrocities? Could the same thing ever happen again, this time in a democratic setting?

As with the other mass murderers, Eichmann's excuse that they were just 'following orders'[30] had a hollow ring to it and seemed a way to justify his involvement in the most despicable of crimes. Was Eichmann just a small cog in the Nazi machinery of death just doing his duty as a loyal Nazi, and if he hadn't completed his duties efficiently he would have been removed or shot? Eichmann had personally visited the concentration camps and had been sickened by what he saw but this had not stopped him from dispatching people that his leaders considered 'sub human'.

Stanley Milgram, a Jewish social psychologist at Yale University, wanted to see how far people were willing to go in obeying authority in a set of obedience tests, which he ran for three years between 1960 and 1963. This revealed some very disturbing results on human compliance. Milgram's experiment would determine if there was something in the German psyche that predisposed them to just 'follow orders' or could a similar situation arise where freedom loving Americans would also cause harm to another if ordered to by an authority figure?

An advert was placed in a local New Haven newspaper[31] as the area was seen as representative of 'small town' America. The advert requested assistance from male volunteers in a scientific study of memory and learning for which they received a small payment of $4.00. Among those requested to attend were labourers, white collar workers and business professionals so that all social strata's of American society were covered. The experiment was to take place at the prestigious Interaction Laboratory at Yale University.

The volunteers arrived two at a time and were greeted by a 'Professor' clothed in a grey lab coat. He explained that the purpose of the experiment would be to see how the introduction of pain affects someone's learning processes. The Professor would be the experimenter while one volunteer would take the place of the teacher, the other the learner.

They drew lots and the learner was taken to a room where in front of the teacher he was strapped to a chair and electrodes placed on his wrists.[32] The teacher was then taken into the next room and introduced to the electric shock generator. The generator had a row of thirty small switches ranging from 15-450 volts in 15 volt increments. Written above the switches were warning signs indicating the levels of shocks that would be administered: *slight - moderate - strong - intensive - extreme intensity - danger - severe shock* - **XXX**.

Before the test started, the experimenter administered a low level shock to the teacher so he could assess what the learner would feel. The teacher spoke to the learner through a microphone asking him to match a series of word pairs from a list. Each time the learner failed to provide a correct answer, an electric shock would be administered. However, unbeknown to the teacher, the test was rigged and the New Haven volunteer would always be the teacher, as the other was Mr Wallace a trained actor.[33] As soon as the door was closed, Mr Wallace undid his straps and placed a tape machine next to a light panel that registered how much the teacher had 'shocked' him. The tape machine would send out a small grunt for a low voltage shock to shouts and screams as the voltage moved further up the scale. As the intensity of the electric shocks reached danger levels, the learner could be heard in the next room crying out in pain, complaining of a bad heart and would plead with his assailant to stop shocking him. The real purpose of the experiment was to see just how much pain one individual was willing to inflict upon another when ordered to, by an authority figure within a certain setting.

When the teacher was given an incorrect answer and hesitated or refused to administer shocks at a higher level, the experimenter used a number of verbal commands to convince him to proceed.[34]

Prompt 1 Please continue or please go on.
Prompt 2 The experiment requires that you continue.
Prompt 3 It is absolutely essential that you continue.
Prompt 4 You have no other choice, you must go on.

Of course, the teacher at any point could have brought the process to an abrupt end by simply refusing to comply with the experimenter's instructions and walk out. However, he suspected that if he did, payment for his participation may have been refused. What is most disturbing is that over 60% of the teachers in the experiment went on to shock the learner at the XXX level, long after he had finished responding to any stimuli from the teacher, who must have considered him either dead or unconscious. A number of participants refused to continue past halfway and confronted the experimenter as they were themselves showing great signs of distress. All the teachers were properly debriefed after each session ended and met with the learner who was very much alive and well. They then had the real purpose of the experiment explained to them.

We see the same psychological 'prompts' being used today to pressurise people to get the Coronavirus vaccination; Threatening loss of income, loss of job, home incarceration, foreign travel ban, suspension of Twitter feeds and YouTube accounts on those who sought or encouraged other remedies. This included vicious personal attacks on the credibility of any scientist who dared to put forward an alternative view.

Chapter 5

Vaccine Tyranny

For someone to give permission for a medical professional to inoculate them with a vaccine requires complete transparency in respect of what ingredients are within each vaccine. The failure of vaccine manufacturers to disclose this information and to coerce an individual to undertake a course of action that may be harmful to them is in breach of the Nuremberg Code. Extensive experiments undertaken by Professor Pablo Compra[35] have found traces of graphite, graphene oxide and reduced graphene oxide in the 110 vaccines he tested from samples he obtained from Pfizer, AstraZeneca, Moderna and Janssen using a Micro-Raman Spectroscope. All samples showed evidence of additional materials that had not been disclosed on company information sheets. Further experiments using Micro-Spectrometry undertaken by Dr. Robert Young,[36] confirmed that undisclosed materials including parasites had been found in the vaccines.

Without spending time studying the complex information on the Pfizer, Moderna or AstraZenica websites, it will be difficult to detect what these companies are using or understand why. Those who are independently testing the contents of the vials and going public are being ridiculed, debunked or 'fact checked.'[37] Graphene oxide has some unusual properties and has been used to revolutionise battery and information technology production. Animal testing has shown that injected graphene can regenerate worn out bone tissue and shrink the size of tumours. However, its nano-particles can also cause fluids to build up in the lungs resulting in the patient 'dry drowning'. There is also a rare possibility of it circumventing the blood/brain barrier as well as disrupting kidneys, which can lead to a painful condition called Nephritic Syndrome where legs and eyes swell up.

When heated, graphene can expand and is shown clumping together and affecting red blood cells. *See picture gallery.* Some people have claimed that their arms have become numb or magnetised after being vaccinated and the graphene may act as some sort of internal tagging device, which may be able to be picked up via hand held devices. Experiments to improve the bioluminescence of Luciferase that glows in the dark and has also been placed in vaccines and how it interacts with human blood cells can be viewed on the Moderna website, under Intellectual Property US Patent 10,898574 B2 *Picture gallery table*[19].

Doctors and Professors using Micro Spectrometry and the Micro-Raman Spectroscope are revealing the truth about the vaccines being offered to the general public. There are absolutely no beneficial or therapeutic reasons why these substances should have been added to our vaccines, and could do us all immeasurable internal damage. Graphene looks like tiny metallic shards and has been described by one expert as being like tiny razor blades. As if this didn't cause enough reason to rethink our position on being vaccinated, ethical doubts on the integrity of these multinationals should be properly investigated. Johnson and Johnson, 'The Family Company,' are currently facing lawsuits of $2.5 billion as a number of distressed parents sue the company as they believe its talcum powder has caused harm and sometimes death to their children.

So that everyone is vaccinated for future tracking purposes, a virus must be manufactured to panic the masses. This also fits in well with the United Nations Agenda 2021 and 2030 depopulation/sustainability objectives. Using the laboratory in Wuhan and having success with SARS-Cov-1 which infected over 8000 without mutating, Dr Sui Zhengli,[38] using gain of function research, developed another bat virus, this time recombining its genes with a pangolin, making it extremely infectious and virulent. However, just before the virus was moved out of China and released elsewhere, it accidently escaped and created awareness world-wide of how many of these dangerous laboratory produced viruses are being developed for biological warfare purposes.

Here is a short transcript of a US Senate Committee meeting on Health, Education, Labour and Pensions held on May 11th 2021 where gain of function was discussed between Senator Rand Paul from Kentucky and Dr. Anthony Fauci, Head of National Institute of Allergy and Infectious Diseases (NIAID):

Paul: 'Dr. Fauci, we don't know whether the pandemic started in a lab in Wuhan or evolved naturally but we should want to know. Gain of function research, as you know, is juicing up naturally occurring animal viruses to infect humans. To arrive at the truth, the US Government should admit that the Wuhan Virology Institute was experimenting to enhance the Coronavirus's ability to infect humans. For years Dr Ralph Barac a virologist in the US has been collaborating with Dr Sui Zhengli of the Wuhan Virology Institute sharing his discoveries about how to create super viruses. Doctors Barac and Sui worked together to insert bat virus spike protein into the backbone of the deadly SARS virus and then used this man made super virus to infect human airway cells. Dr. Fauci, do you still support NIH funding of the Lab in Wuhan?'

Fauci: 'We do not send money now to Wuhan Virology...'

Paul: 'We did under your tutelage; we were sending it through Eco Health. It was a sub agency and a sub grant. There was research done with Dr Sui and Dr Barac. They have collaborated on gain of function research where they enhanced the SARS virus to infect human airways cells and they did it by merging a new spike protein on it. That is gain of function. That was joint research between the Wuhan Institute and Dr Barac - you can't deny it!'

Paul: 'You're fooling with Mother Nature here. You're allowing super viruses to be created with a 15% mortality. It's very dangerous and it was a huge mistake to share this with China and it's a huge mistake to allow this to continue in the United States and we should be very careful to investigate where this virus came from.'

Not only has dangerous materials been placed in our Covid vaccines, it has also been found in our Influenza shots.[39] These contain thimerosal, which is toxic through inhalation, ingestion or skin contact, formaldehyde (or formalin), chicken kidney cells and DNA, monosodium glutamate, Oxtoxynol-9 (Triton X-100) used in spermicides and polysorbate 80 (which caused an anaphylactic reaction in a German patient). In the UK, three vaccine manufacturers faced prosecution after the administration of the MMR (mumps, measles and rubella) vaccine, which, according to the 1,500 parents, had caused significant changes in their children, including autism and bowel problems. However, in 2003 as medical reports were being prepared, the UK Government withdrew legal aid[40] from the parents and the case subsequently collapsed, leaving devastated parents without the financial means to continue and the case unresolved.

There seems to be a rolling programme of inventing new viruses and then tweaking them to target certain 'people groups' that are thought to be ' breeding too quickly.' This is particularly evident in Black Asian and Minority Ethnic communities (B.A.M.E)[41] and Learning Disability Communities.[42] Those that are from an ethnic background generally have less natural vitamin D, which alongside zinc has been shown to increase natural immunity. People with a learning disability are more than six times more likely to become infected with Covid than the rest of the population, whereas the death rate for those with a learning disability aged 18-34 are over thirty times higher than the rest of the population.

In England 94% of Covid deaths are now from those who have been triple vaccinated.[43] The death rate for those aged 10-14 is now 52 times higher than pre-inoculation levels. Previously fit and healthy young people are finding themselves struggling with Myocarditis and other heart related issues. Since March, figures on child deaths/injury are no longer being produced by the N.H.S. Information from the Medicines and Healthcare Products Agency updated on 01/09/2022, gave a breakdown on how many adverse reactions, some serious, have been reported in the UK from each individual provider

Pfizer-BioNTech UK Including Northern Ireland - 159,013
AstraZeneca UK Including Northern Ireland - 234,095
Moderna UK Including Northern Ireland - 38,340
Supplies of the AstraZeneca vaccine are very quietly being phased out.

To ensure the virus bandwagon keeps moving forward, in 2010 the US Government patented all Ebola viruses that share 70% similarity or more of the Ebola strain. Patent information sheets declare the owners are: The Government of The United States of America as represented by the Secretary; Department of Health and Human Services; The Centre for

Disease Control, Patent CA2741523A1. Other medications that have been proven to work with early treatment against Coronavirus like Budesonide, Hydroxychloroquine and Ivermectin are being belittled by the medical professionals that are promoting the Globalist's agenda.

Then there are the medical 'experts' that press the panic button telling us that this particular virus will be as bad as the Spanish Flu, and that catastrophe lies ahead for the unvaccinated. Billions are spent developing vaccines which are oversupplied and then discarded as they come to the end of their natural life. The pharmaceutical companies have riches beyond avarice while even more funds are siphoned away from national governments.

To check how easily people have been manipulated to take the vaccine, I have included a short complicity test:

1) You believe everything the Government has told you about the coronavirus and you must take a recommended vaccine to reduce your risk of transmission.
2) You believe that if there was another available treatment for the virus, rather than the recommended Pfizer, AstraZeneca, Moderna, or Johnson and Johnson vaccines, your GP would have told you.
3) You believe that anti-vaxxers are a bunch of conspiracy theorists that have rejected a proven scientific approach to treating the virus.
4) You believe that you don't need to waste time researching alternative treatments as your Government has got your best interests at heart.
5) You believe that most of the reported vaccine injuries are extremely rare and that a lot of the stories circulating on the internet are 'fake news.'
6) You believe that pharmaceutical companies have high moral and ethical standards and they put people before profit.

7) You believe that the NHS did not put "Do Not Resuscitate" orders on people's beds unnecessarily.

8) You believe that everyone over five years old should take the vaccine as a precaution.

9) You believe that it is the unvaccinated that are spreading the virus and that the Government should take stringent action to isolate them.

10) You believe that the vaccine should be mandatory and that the people who refuse it should be marginalised from society and fined for 'non compliance.'

As Luciferase has a 'half life', it needs to be boosted every year to remain effective, and therefore increases the risk of serious vaccine injuries taking place. The 'Vaccine Apocalypse' is yet to be fully realised. The term Luciferase is derived from the name of Lucifer himself. Therefore this is not just a human plan; it is a satanic plot to prepare the world for the revealing of the man of sin that the Bible calls the Antichrist.

Chapter 6

Gain of Function Research

Anyone wanting further evidence of man's foolish and remorseless ability to sow the seeds of his own destruction need to look no further than the U.S. Government supported gain of function research. This is a euphemism for biological research aimed at *increasing* the virulence and lethality of pathogens and viruses. This includes enhancing the pathogen's ability to infect different species and to increase their deadly impact as *airborne* pathogens and viruses. In 2011 the National Science Advisory Board for Bio-Security[44] was able to increase the transmissibility of the H5NI virus between ferrets, changing its pathway into one that included airborne transmission.

After a number of dangerous lab leaks took place, gain of function research was suspended for a few years. However, on 19th December 2017, the US National Institute For Health announced that they would be restarting GOF research into Middle East Respiratory Syndrome (MERS), the flu virus, coronavirus and the Severe Acute Respiratory virus (SARS).

The excuse that we have to mutate viruses and dangerous pathogens to find cures in case hostile governments, groups or individuals threaten to release genetically enhanced viruses on humanity, should become a new definition for madness. This new breed of bio-weapons are being developed to cause 'mass infection' as the release of the highly contagious SARS-Cov-2 virus from the lab in Wuhan proves.

Not only are these new bio-weapons a 'clear and present danger' to us all, it would appear that their virulence has been increased to target certain racial groups and vulnerable adults. Remember the Genome project had a particular focus on identifying different ethnic groupings susceptibility to disease. It only takes a bit of 'outside the box' thinking to conclude that this particular virus has been tweaked and used as a depopulation tool to dispose of those who the New World Order considered to have an inferior genetic code.

Articles in a number of newspapers in July 2020 revealed that the use of Midazolam in hospitals had dramatically increased from February to April, as had the number of 'Do Not Resuscitate' orders placed on hospital and care home files.[45] Although Midazolam is a legitimate drug for end of life care, it can also suppress breathing and can therefore sometimes be fatal if prescribed inappropriately.[46] Retired neurologist, Professor Patrick Pullicino, raised concerns that the Liverpool Care Pathway was already accelerating people's deaths using official flow charts that had identified those deemed too frail for end of life care.[47] The Care Quality Commission received forty submissions from the public, mostly about DNACPR (Do Not Attempt Cardiopulmonary Resuscitation) orders placed on their loved one's beds without consultation with either their family or the person involved. This led to the suspicion that a form of 'back door' euthanasia was being administered. No-one has the right to determine who lives and who dies unless it is to reduce severe suffering, which should be a conversation had between the medical professionals and the individual's family and their other support networks.

When you had the MMR vaccine as a child, how many second doses or booster shots did you need? None! You knew that the treatment was effective and long lasting. You knew you would have lifetime immunity. The need to constantly re-vaccinate the populace against the latest strains of the virus can lead us to only one conclusion - that all the current vaccines on offer are 'leaky.' A leaky vaccine is one that reduces the effects of the disease on the vaccinated individual but then uses their host to shed the virus to others, including those already vaccinated, leading to the false premise that if you are double vaccinated and boosted it is safe to attend venues and be in close proximity with others. These gatherings became major 'shedding events' with some catching covid two or three times after being vaccinated. If the vaccine really worked, then how could people catch it from the unvaccinated, who at the time, were excluded from these events?

Studies have been undertaken in regard to Marek's disease[48] which badly affects the chicken population causing paralysis and death. In this study, two sets of chickens with the disease were separated with one group being vaccinated and the other left unvaccinated. Uninfected chickens were then introduced to these two groups. What the study found was that the vaccinated chickens harboured a huge viral load of the virus and leaked hotter, more dangerous, strains to the unvaccinated chickens, which subsequently died.

Peer-reviewed studies found that people who caught the Spanish Flu still had anti-bodies which prevented further infection eighty years[49] after the 1918 pandemic as did those who became unwell with Sars-Cov-1, years after the initial outbreak took place. Why would anyone try to convince someone who had caught Sars-Cov-2 and had built up natural immunity to then swap it for a potentially leaky vaccine that had been shown to lose its strength over time and needs constant boosting to maintain its effectiveness?

Pfizer's stage 3 trials which were initially meant to run for three years stopped after only two months of testing when the blind trial group were then un-blinded and offered the Pfizer inoculation, which most agreed to.[50] However, since most of the placebo group had now changed over to the vaccinated group; no further trial data about the effectiveness of the vaccine could be properly evaluated.

Pfizer's patchy past performance in developing and promoting potentially dangerous products should also give us cause for concern[51].

1) Faulty heart valves – Pfizer's subsidiary company Shiley Inc., sold heart valves between 1976 and 1979 with 55,000 receiving the implant. In the mid 1980's, the FDA issued a recall after it was discovered that the valve had a tendency to fracture. By 1991, 450 heart valves had failed, leading to the deaths of 350 people. Warning letters were sent out to 20,000 patients who had received the implant. Pfizer's CEO at that time, said that the claims 'lacked merit' but agreed to pay out $215 million to end the lawsuit.

2) Trovan – Launched 2009 and trialled in Nigeria as an experimental anti meningitis drug. This drug was cited as causing eleven children's deaths, the rest being left with brain damage, blindness, deafness and paralysis. Pfizer agreed to pay compensation of $75 million.

3) Rapamune - The drug was used to reduce the rejection of kidneys in transplant patients, which the FDA granted approval of in 1999. Wreath, a subsidiary of Pfizer, then marketed the drug to patients who received different organ transplants and gave 'financial incentives' for its use. Pleading guilty of misbranding, they agreed to a final financial settlement amounting to $490.9 million. An amount of $257.4 million was set aside for civil settlements while the rest was procured for criminal fines.

4) In September 2009, an ABC News article reported on 'The Greatest Health Care Fraud Settlement in History' when

Pfizer's subsidiary companies Pharmacia and Upjohn Inc. were fined an eye-watering $2.3 billion for illegally promoting, without FDA approval, Geodin, Lyrica, Zyvax and Bextra, and providing financial kick-backs for their use.

On 30th April 2021 Pfizer finally released its report 5.3.6. CUMULATIVE ANALYSIS OF POST-AUTHORISATION ADVERSE EVENT REPORTS OF PF07302048 (BNT162B2). This was from the onset of the vaccine being administered through to 28/02/2021. In this report it acknowledges there have been over 1,400 confirmed different side effects, some serious or fatal that had resulted from its coronavirus vaccine. That's not 1,400 people, but 1,400 different types of vaccine injuries that have taken place. From acquired epileptic aphasia to Zica virus associated Guillain Barre Syndrome, this document reads like the medical dictionary from HELL!

Each section is broken down into different sub sections. The section on page 19 mentions facial paralysis. Number of cases - 449 with 399 designated as serious; US cases 124 - UK cases 119. The rest are mainly in Europe. Although these individuals have experienced horrific and presumably permanent life changing injuries, Pfizer's lack of human compassion for its victims is evident in this closing paragraph – 'Overall Conclusion: The cumulative case review does not raise new safety concerns. Surveillance will continue.' It's as though Pfizer expected this level of injury would occur when it manufactured its vaccine.

Before you continue reading this book, would you put the '5.3.6. reference' in your search engine for careful consideration. It's only when you read this bombshell document and question why no major news outlets have reported on its findings, that you will begin to understand the dishonesty and deception being deployed by world governments to prevent the general public from making properly informed choices on managing their health regimes.

Just imagine the joy of the Pfizer's Managing Directors when, with their history of unethical work practices and litigation through the courts, the American Government provided them with the ability to produce and distribute their experimental anti-coronavirus drugs without accountability. All this while hundreds of thousands of voiceless individuals who are suffering vaccine injury are ignored by the media and receive no financial compensation to assist with their lack of income. Their cases are seldom heard due to the New World Order's control of our airwaves.

Chapter 7

The Origins of Evil

The Bible tells us that the originator of sin, wickedness and deception is Satan himself. He not only fell from God's grace by being lifted up with pride, he took one third of the angels with him. People who have rejected Christianity or have limited knowledge of biblical prophecy will not fully understand that the Bible has a lot to say about spiritual beings - how they have affected our past and how they will be shaping our future.

One of the first direct references to Lucifer (the name means light bearer) is in Isaiah 14:12-15. He had a prominent role in Heaven and appears to be involved in Heaven's music ministry. He became lifted up with pride and rebelled against his Creator. 'How you are fallen from Heaven, O Day Star, son of Dawn! How you are cut down to the ground, you who laid the nations low! You said in your heart, 'I will ascend to heaven; I will raise my throne above the stars (angels) of God; I will sit on the mount of assembly on the heights of Zaphon; I will ascend to the tops of the clouds, I will make myself like the Most High.' God's retort to Satan was, 'But you shall be brought down to Sheol to the depths of the Pit.' Realising that he couldn't gain ascendency over God he did the next best thing - attack God's creation. By influencing and then speaking through the mouth of a serpent, he caused Adam and Eve to sin and at that point he became their legitimate ruler and by default ours! His name was changed by God to Satan, which means adversary, and he was thrown out of the heavenly realms. He now operates as the 'Prince of the Power of the Air'. This also includes all our airwaves!

After the fall of Satan and a third of God's angels were corrupted and thrown out of Heaven, a second angelic rebellion took place in the ancient world. This is referenced in Genesis 6 and explained in more detail in the book of Enoch, which is the most ancient and prominent non-biblical wisdom literature books in circulation. The Bible informs us that the sons of God (the angels) lusted over the daughters of Eve and decided to sire children themselves. God was angry with the angels and the devastating effects their sin was having on humanity and he reduced mankind's longevity. The sixth chapter of Enoch informs us that two hundred angels made a pact on Mount Hermon in the days of Jared, Enoch's Father. They all agreed to leave their spiritual abode, materialise on the earth and become parents.

Enoch 6:1 + 7:6 'And all the (angels) took unto themselves wives and each chose for himself one and they begun to go in unto them and defile themselves with them, and they taught them charms and enchantments and the cutting of roots, (drug addiction/love potions) and made them acquainted with plants (homeopathy) and their women became pregnant and they bare great giants... who consumed all the acquisitions of men and when men could no longer sustain them, the giants turned against them and devoured mankind. And they begun to sin against birds and beasts and reptiles and fish and to devour one another's flesh and drink the blood. And the earth laid accusations against the lawless ones.'

The angels revealed occult secrets to humanity, and their 'children' were born as a race of mutated giants that became known as the Nephelim, which means fallen. The ring leaders of this rebellion were two fallen angels called Azazel and Semjaza.

Enoch 8:1-4: 'And Azazel taught men to make swords, and knives, and shields, and breastplates, and taught them about metals of the earth and the art of working them, and bracelets, and ornaments, and the use of antimony, and the beautifying of the eyelids, and all kinds of precious stones, and all colouring and dyes. And there was great impiety; they turned away from God, and committed fornication, and they were led astray and became corrupt in all their ways. And as men perished, they cried, and their cry went up to Heaven.'

Jasher 2:19-20 'For in those days the sons of men began to trespass against God, and to go contrary to the commandments which he had given Adam, to be prolific and reproduce in the earth. And some of the sons of men caused their wives to drink a mixture that would render them unable to conceive, in order that they might retain their figures and their beautiful appearance might not fade.'

Jasher 4:18 'And their judges and rulers went to the daughters of men and took their wives by force from their husbands according to their choice, and the sons of men in those days took from the cattle of the earth, the beasts of the field and the fowls of the air, and taught the mixture of animals of one species with the other, in order therewith to provoke the Lord; and God saw the whole earth and it was corrupt, for all flesh had corrupted its ways on earth, all men and all animals.'

When the Dead Sea Scrolls were discovered in 1947, they found lost manuscript fragments from Enoch in Qumran, in cave 4 in very poor condition but also fragments from The Book of Giants in caves 1, 2, 3 and 6. This contained information on the cross-breeding of different species during the reign of Nimrod. IQ23 Fragment 1-6, two hundred asses... two hundred rams... two hundred goats... two hundred... (beasts of the field) from every animal and every bird for miscegenation. Perhaps some of the strange creatures represented in Egyptian hieroglyphs were not just mythical creatures after all!

Chapter 8

God's Judgement on the Fallen Angels

The cohabitation between angels and women caused mankind dire consequences. Because angels are spiritual in nature, every time one of the angel's giant 'children' died, a demonic spirit that cannot physically die was released on the earth. Their mission is to attack, oppress, control, possess and destroy human life and will remain here until Christ returns to cleanse the earth.

The book of Enoch confirms how these demonic forces operate: 'And the spirits of the giants afflict, attack, oppress, do battle, and work destruction on the earth and cause trouble: they take no food (but nevertheless) hunger and thirst and cause offences. And these spirits will rise up against the children of men because they have proceeded from them.' (Enoch 15:11)

God sent Enoch to inform the fallen angels, that through Noah's flood, they would witness the destruction of their progeny. (Enoch 12:6) After the flood, they were imprisoned in a gloomy dungeon called Tartarus, but not before the angels had started procreating with postdiluvian women again. God ascribed all of this sin to Azazel (Enoch 10:8) as he was the main proponent of this rebellion. However, he was not sent to Tartarus but chained up in the wilderness and appears to be connected to the Jewish 'Day Of Atonement Sacrifice.'

Leviticus 16:6, 'And Aaron shall offer the bull as a sin offering for himself and for his house. He shall then take the two goats and set them before the Lord at the door at the tent of meeting and Aaron shall cast lots upon the two goats -one lot for the Lord and the other lot for Azazel. And Aaron shall present the goat on which the lot fell for the Lord and offer it as a sin offering. But the goat on which the lot fell for Azazel shall be presented alive to make atonement over it that it may be sent away into the wilderness to Azazel. This is the only time a goat is specifically offered for Jewish sacrifices. We can only assume that God's Holy Spirit led the poor bleating goat to his chained up namesake who was languishing somewhere in the wilderness as an annual reminder of the terrible sin he had committed against the Lord.

Jesus explained how demons operate and desire human contact and habitation. Matt 12:43, 'When an unclean spirit is gone out of a person, it wanders through waterless regions looking for a resting place, but it finds none. Then it says, "I will return to my house from which I came." When it comes, it finds it empty, swept, and put in order. It then goes and brings along seven other spirits more evil than itself, and they enter and live there; and the last state of that person is worse than the first.' Unless the individual is truly repentant and turns away from their sin they may find themselves open to re-possession.

With most people ignoring God today, it's not surprising that dark forces have gained a foothold and made inroads into people's lives. Invisible demonic entities are feeding on our weaknesses, driving people to use drugs, gamble, get into debt, smoke, become an alcoholic, commit adultery and ultimately kill themselves. Demons hate water because it reminds them of Noah's flood. When someone is baptised with full immersion in Christ's name, they are declaring to the principalities and powers that they are cut off from the old world and being raised in newness of life. As Jesus gave power to the disciples to exorcise demons, he also gives his born again Church power over all the works of the enemy. It's only when you are born again and empowered by God's Holy Spirit that you have authority over these demonic beings. Matthew 10:1.

Jesus warned us that at the end of the world, society would strongly resemble the days in which Noah lived. Paul's second letter to Timothy 3:1-4 describes the 'human condition' just before Christ's return. 'You must understand this, that in the last days distressing times will come. For people will be lovers of themselves, lovers of money, boasters, arrogant, abusive, disobedient to their parents, ungrateful, unholy, inhuman, implacable, slanderers, profligates, brutes, haters of good, treacherous, reckless, swollen with conceit, lovers of pleasure rather than lovers of God.'

What better description could you give on today's world than the one above? Development of weapons of warfare, murder, lack of respect for human life, increase in witchcraft, curses, forced sterilisation, abortion, sexual and financial exploitation of the poor by the rich, slavery and the cross fertilisation of animals. God made each animal after *its own kind*. The result in this rebellion ended in Noah's flood. The judgement of this *current world* will end up with a worldwide famine; asteroid's falling from the sky and the battle of Armageddon. The final conflict of this age will be between Jesus Christ with his returning saints and Satan, the false prophet, the Antichrist and his New World Order.

Chapter 9

Nimrod, the Tower of Babel
and the First Global Governance

Jasher 9:20-34

'And King Nimrod reigned securely, and all the earth was under his control, and all the earth was of one tongue and words of union. And all the princes of Nimrod and his great men took counsel together; Phut, Mitzraim, Cush and Canaan with their families, and they said to each other, "Come, let us build ourselves a city and in it a strong tower, and its top reaching Heaven, and we will make ourselves famed, so that we may reign upon the whole world, in order that evil of our enemies may cease from us, that we may reign mightily over them, and that we may not become scattered over the earth on account of their wars." And they all went before the king and they told the king these words, and the king agreed with them in this affair, and he did so.

And all the families assembled, consisting of about six hundred thousand men, and they went to seek an extensive piece of ground to build the city and the tower, and they sought in the whole earth and they found none like one valley at the east of the land of Shinar, about two days walk, and they journeyed there and they dwelt there. And they began to make bricks and burn fires to build the city and the tower that they had imagined to complete. And the building of the tower was unto them a transgression and a sin, and they began to build it, and whilst they were building against the Lord God of Heaven, they imagined in their hearts to war against him and to ascend into Heaven. And all these people and all the families divided themselves in three parts; the first said, "We will ascend into Heaven and fight against him;" the second said, "We will ascend to Heaven and place our own gods there and serve them;" and the third part said, "We will ascend to Heaven and smite him with bows and spears;" and God knew all their works and all their evil thoughts, and he saw the city and the tower, which they were building. And when they were building they built themselves a great city and a very high and strong tower; and on account of its height, the mortar and bricks did not reach the builders in their ascent to it, until those who went up had completed a full day, and after that, they reached to the builders and gave them the mortar and the bricks; thus was it done daily. And behold these ascended and others descended the whole day; and if a brick should fall from their hands and get broken, they would all weep over it; and if a man fell and died, none would look at him.

And the Lord knew their thoughts, and it came to pass when they were building, they cast the arrows toward the heavens, and all the arrows fell upon them filled with blood, and when they saw them they said to each other, "Surely, we have slain all those that are in Heaven. For this was from the Lord in order to cause them to err, and in order to destroy them from off the face of the ground." And they built the tower and the city, and they did this thing daily until many days and years were elapsed. And God said to the seventy angels who stood foremost before him, to those who were near to him, saying, "Come, let us descend and confuse their tongues, that one man shall not understand the language of his neighbour," and they did so unto them. And from that day following, they forgot each man his neighbour's tongue, and they could not understand to speak in one tongue, and when the builder took from the hands of his neighbour lime or stone, which he did not order, the builder would cast it away and throw it upon his neighbour, that he would die. And they did so many days, and they killed many of them in this manner.'

The book of Jasher also provides us with further information on the translation of Enoch and why God hated Noah's son Ham. Just like Elijah, Enoch was also translated into Heaven via a whirlwind in a fiery chariot with spirit horses and fire. They will both return to earth as the two end time prophets who witness in Jerusalem and bring God's judgement on the earth at the time of the Antichrist. (Revelation 11:1-13)

Jasher 3:35-36, 'And they, (Enoch's followers) urged so much to go with him, that he ceased speaking to them; and they went after him and would not return; and when the kings returned, they caused a census to be taken, in order to know the number of remaining men that went with Enoch; and it was on the seventh day that Enoch ascended into Heaven in a whirlwind with horses and chariots of fire.'

The garments that had been given to Adam and Eve by God and handed to Noah were stolen by Ham, (Jasher 7:27-28) and were secretly given to Cush his son, who then handed them over to Nimrod as they were thought to have special powers.

Chapter 10

The New World Order and the Second Global Governance

'We now see a new world coming into view. A world where there is a real prospect of a New World Order.' Speech by George Bush, March 6th 1991.

To understand how our society has become extraordinarily financially unbalanced, and how more and more money is being transferred into fewer and fewer hands, you need to gain a historical perspective.[52] The Constantinople letter dated 22nd December 1489 provided a blueprint for a number of Elite bankers on how a democratic society could be influenced, infiltrated and eventually subjugated by a group of determined individuals. To implement this blueprint would require a brotherhood to be formed.[53] This group of powerful and unscrupulous men first met secretly in the 1530's in Spain, where they became the 'Brotherhood of the Illuminati.' Their aim on 'how to conquer the leadership of the world' was the basis of the meeting of influential families that took place in 1773, after which Mayer Amschel Rothschild commented, 'If we combine our forces we can control the world.'[54]

Those who have commented on this elaborate conspiracy have also rightly identified 1776 as the year that Jesuit Professor Adam Weishaupt, who worked at the Jesuit University in Ingolstadt Bavaria, also founded the German order of the Illuminati of Enlightened Ones.[55] Weishaupt's movement soon attracted a number of powerful European families and became a clandestine force within German society. In 1784 an attempted coup against the Hapsburgs was foiled and the Illuminati were forced underground and started to infiltrate Masonic Lodges.

In 1923 a number of 'illuminated' prominent banking families achieved a huge breakthrough by taking control of the Federal Reserve.[56] This gave a small group of banking conspiritors ultimate control over the American economy and influence over world events. John Franklin Kennedy understood, but underestimated, the dangers of an unfettered CIA and Federal Reserve. Kennedy declared that he would 'splinter the C.I.A. into a thousand pieces and scatter it to the wind.'[57] In an attempt to transfer power away from the Federal Reserve and place it into the hands of the US Department Of The Treasury, on June 4th 1963, Kennedy issued $4 billion worth of Treasury Notes. These were underpinned by silver, and interest free. The issuing of silver certificates to Americans gave an intrinsic value to the US dollar. A few months later JFK was assassinated and the certificates were withdrawn.

The Elite control the five Companies that nearly control all 'independent news' media outlets.[58] These are; Disney Corporation, Time Warner, Sony, News Corp and National Amusements. These organisations are worth an estimated $430 billion, and they ensure that all news is carefully screened before broadcasting or publication takes place.

It is not possible within the scope of this book to document all the treacherous historical undertakings of these mendacious collaborators, however, I have produced a short watch list of the families, groups, organisations and educational institutions that are financed, controlled or have ties to the secret brotherhood. These people are without any human compassion, and desire to depopulate the earth and turn those remaining into a breed of micro-chipped AI enhanced chimera worker drones.

The main dynasties[59] that today control nearly all the levers of world power, banking and industry, are, in fact, thirteen satanic family bloodlines, consisting of: Warburg, Rothschild, Rockefeller, Dupont, Russell, Onassis, Collins, Morgan, Kennedy, Hapsburg, Li, Bundy and Astor. The second tier of families who work in partnership with these families at the top of the pyramid, are Vanderbilt, Bauer, Witney, Oppenheimer, Sassoon, Wheeler, Todd, Clinton, Taft, Goldschmidt, Wallenberg, Guggenheim, Bush and other prominent families.

The Bilderburger Group.[60] Since its inception, this secret group of powerful individuals, who first met at the Hotel de Bilderburg in 1954 in the small Dutch town of Oosterbeek, have continued to promote and carry out the Globalists agenda. The group has almost become a who's who of the rich and powerful and includes Political leaders, Industrialists, Bankers and Influencers. Meetings take place once a year at different locations around the world, and are held in complete secrecy. At every meeting, roads are sealed off and are surrounded by military clad armed police.

The World Economic Forum, led by Klaus Schwab.[61] The WEF has moved from the periphery to become a major player, which will very soon shape future events, and is working to destroy our cash based current financial system and replace it with 'The Great Reset.' This is a new financial model based on Central Bank Digital Currencies. Schwab does not hide the fact that the world will not be allowed to return to its pre-pandemic state, and he links financial changes to a future planned change in human biology. People will lose the right to own their own property. Everything will be kept in safe-keeping by the Elite who will lease you everything. (See picture gallery poster) It is not surprising then that the head of the Chinese Government Xi Jinping has spoken at WEF events via a video link.

In an interview in 2017[63] Schwab boasted that those who support the Forum's Globalist Agenda have 'infiltrated into the highest levels of all world Governments.' Their next step is to set up 'Global Food Innovation Hubs,' which will 'transform food systems and land use.' One great supporter of this initiative is the Dutch PM Mark Rutte[64] who is in charge of the inappropriately named, 'The People's Party for Freedom and Democracy.' Rutte has insisted that Dutch Farmers must reduce the nitrogen ammonia content in the soil, from between 30-70% to reach agreed targets to reduce 'Greenhouse gases' by 2030, or they will lose their farms.

If they implement this target throughout Europe, thousands of farmers, some who are currently protesting to protect their livelihoods in the Netherlands, will be turfed off their land over the next seven years due to artificially inflated animal feed costs, and Agenda 2030 'sustainability' objectives.[64] The 'Climate Emergency' is again being used as a tool of oppression, this time to reduce the amount of food in production. These restraints on production will keep escalating food prices and eventually develop into a planned worldwide famine, with Globalists in charge of the worlds' 'food banks.'

Bohemian Club/Grove. Created in 1872 in San Francisco,[65] The Bohemian Club initially attracted poets, playwrights, artists and artisans who had became part of the avant-garde movement but then became infiltrated by others, with quite a different agenda. Amongst those who have attended Bohemian events, are Presidents Ronald Reagan, Richard Nixon and George Bush, along with other luminaries like publisher Randolph Hearst, Henry Kissinger and former National Security Agency Director, Bobby Ray Inman. Those running this secretive 'culture club' have taken it to a very different direction than its original founder's egalitarian vision.

Members of the Bohemian Club[66] meet annually for seventeen days in July at a remote 'sacred grove' in a 30,000 acre compound in Sinoma County California, which is surrounded by redwood trees. Access is denied to the general public. This is where a ceremony known as the 'Cremation of the Care' takes place in front of a forty foot Owl that resembles the Canaanite god Molech, where, historically, child sacrifices took place.

The Club of Rome[67] was created in 1968 by the Montentheu Group during a meeting at the Rockefeller's private house in Bellagio Italy. In 1973, the Club published a report entitled, 'The Regionalised and Adaptive Model of the Global World System.' The report revealed the Club's intention, through regionalisation, to divide the world into ten economic and political regions called Kingdoms, uniting the world under a 'common leadership.' The different regions are: North America ~ Western Europe ~ Eastern Europe ~ Japan ~ The rest of the Developed World ~ Latin America ~ The Middle East ~ The rest of Africa ~ South and South East Asia - China. This model has now been adopted by the United Nations.[68]

The World Health Organisation founded on 7th April 1948 in Geneva. The WHO is a specialised agency of the United Nations. Its constitution states its objectives are to, 'Raise the attainment of all peoples of the highest possible level of health.' It has six Regional and 150 field offices around the world. The main funders of the WHO are Germany 12.8%, The Bill and Melinda Gates Foundation 11.65% and the United States 7.85%.[69]

However, recent controversies on how the WHO is being run have called into question its independence. It is accused of being unduly influenced by China. The WHO's unwillingness to declare coronavirus a pandemic until 11th March 2020, by which time it had already travelled half way round the world, caused concern. So did the sycophantic efforts by the WHO's leaders, in their attempt to find an alternative narrative to the blindingly obvious, that the virus escaped from the lab in Wuhan during its gain of function research. This caused President Trump to start proceedings to defund the organisation, insisting that it was too deferential to the Chinese Government. This decision was reversed by the Biden administration.

Chapter 11

CERN's Hadron Collider
and the Bottomless Pit

The very first particle accelerator was invented by Sir John Douglas Cockford and Irish Physicist Ernest Walton. They used the accelerator to split the atom on April 14th 1932, for which they received the Nobel Prize in physics for their work on 'the transmutation of the atomic nuclei by artificially accelerated atomic particles.'

Recent technological breakthroughs have allowed scientists to gain a huge leap forward in their supposed understanding into the origins of our Universe. No restrictions will be placed on these scientists to prevent them extending their knowledge, even if their experiments contain potentially dangerous risks for the rest of us. Located between France and Switzerland, CERN's seventeen mile underground particle accelerator, called the Hadron Collider, is one controversial development that has split scientific opinion, and for good reason. It was placed at Saint-Genis-Pouilly, which used to be called Appollyiacumis, where an ancient temple dedicated to Apollo used to reside.[70]

In 2004, a large statue of a dancing form of Shiva called a Natarig was unveiled at CERN's Geneva Headquarters.[71] Shiva is one of the triune 'gods' of Hinduism. In Hindu teaching, Brahma is the god of creation; Vishnu is the god of preservation, while Shiva is the god that destroys the world. Shiva's dance of creation and destruction is called the Anandatandava. How strange that atheist physicists, who reject the very idea of God creating the heavens and the earth, would allow a religious statue of a 'god' on their site that in Hindu mythology dances as it destroys the Universe.

The Hadron Collider started its experiments on September 10th 2008, accelerating particles at just under the speed of light, and then smashing them together.[72] The aim of the experiment was to assist scientists to potentially go back in time to understand what conditions were like in our Universe, when particles were in their unformed or unglued state, just before the 'Big Bang' took place. In 2012, CERN scientists discovered the Higgs Boson or 'God Particle.' On the CERN website it states, 'The Higgs Boson can be a *unique portal* to finding signs of dark matter due to its own distinct characteristics and properties.' Regardless of what the website states, CERN are already mining dark matter, which is a by-product of their particle smashing experiments. The Higgs Boson is believed to be a 'passport' particle, which opens extra dimensions, parallel universes and black holes.

Revelation 9:1-11 explains that just before Jesus Christ's return to earth, an angel is given power to open the Bottomless Pit, releasing a hoard of demonic scorpion hybrids upon the earth. The pain is so excruciating from the demonic locusts sting that mankind will seek to die but they will not be able to. This is because by taking the devil's mark they have been changed to chimeras and have their DNA mixed with animal and insect DNA and will find it hard to die. The locusts have a king over them, the angel of the Abyss, whose name in Hebrew is Abaddon and in Greek, Apollyon. The Hadron Collider will open the very gates to Hell itself.

Sometime in the near future, the Hadron Collider will open a portal and release demonic creatures that will torment humanity for five months. It will also open a portal to a third 'beast' who will return to earth half way through the Apocalypse - more on this later.

In 2015, an upgrade to the Hadron Collider was completed, which increased its power exponentially. Just before the re-launch, Stephen Hawkins sounded a warning that at greater power the Hadron Collider had the potential of destroying the Universe, as at higher speeds the collider could become unstable.[73] Other scientists put the possibility of it destroying the earth at 12 to1. However, Hawkins and other scientists' warnings were completely ignored and the experiments continued.

Just before the opening ceremony to celebrate the Hadron Collider's upgrade in 2015, a bizarre filmed presentation from an opera company called Symmetry took place.[74] In front of the Collider, men and women in blue hard hats and white shirts looked around in wonder, danced the Anandatandava and spun round in circles while a workman's watch went back in time. A black hand then opened the man's eyes and he pushed against some white veils and then started to fall through space. The next scene showed him stumbling towards a white circle in a barren wasteland. Within the circle was a dark clothed sinister figure. A workman then found himself within the circle and he danced Shiva's dance of creation and destruction again. Before the film ended, the word 'Symmetry' appeared on screen. (Symmetry is a theoretical condition that could arrive in the near future when a synthesis of several powerful new technologies will radically change the realities in which we find ourselves in an unpredictable manner.) https://www.britannica.com

It is theoretically possible that when particles are smashed together at high speeds, mass and energy become interchangeable, and this provides the opportunity for miniscule black holes to form.[75]

Commenting on the work of CERN, Dr Sergio Burtolucci, the Director for Research and Computing, confirmed that inter-dimensional wormholes were being formed.[76] 'Out of this door might come something, or we could send something through it.' He went on to explain, 'that this dimensional door would open but even with the power of the Hadron Collider, it could only stay open for a small time lapse of 10-26 seconds, but during this infinitesimal amount of time, 'we would be able to peer into this open door, either by getting something out of it or sending something into it.' Burtolucci concluded, 'after this very small time lapse, the door would again shut bringing us back to our fourth dimensional world.'

Chapter 12

Changes Taking Place to the Authorised King James Bible

'Once you have eliminated the impossible, then whatever remains, however improbable, must be the truth. I, however do not like to eliminate the impossible.' – Sherlock Holmes

Is it possible that a colleague of Burtolucci has sent a copy of the King James Bible through the Collider's 'worm-hole' to 'beings' on the other side, as there have been some changes in the AV that are extremely hard to fathom? Here are just some: In the introduction to the Cambridge Authorised Version, King James has been demoted to 'Prince' James. This is not a printing glitch as the wording has been supernaturally changed after publication (see picture gallery).This change even goes as far back as the earliest printed bibles. Just imagine King James' reaction in being presented with a Bible that demoted him to a Prince! Further changes are as follows;

In Genesis chapter one, God only makes one Heaven; singular not heavens!

The Ten Commandments, written on tablets of stone, are now written on tables. Exodus 32:15 'And Moses turned and went down from the mount and the tables of the testimony were in his hand: the *tables* were written on both their sides; on the one side and on the other were they written. And the *tables* were the work of God. Verse 19, 'And it came to pass as he came nigh unto the camp that he saw the calf, and the dancing; and Moses' anger waxed hot and he cast the *tables* out of his hands and break them under the mount.'

Moses and the Ark! Exodus 2:3 'And when she could not longer hide him (Moses) she took for him an *ark* of bulrushes, and daubed it with slime and with pitch and put the child therein; and she laid it in the flags by the rivers brink.'

Compare this rendering with the New Revised Standard Version: 'When she could hide him no longer she got a papyrus basket for him, and plastered it with bitumen and pitch; she put the child in it and placed it among the reeds on the bank of the river.'

Isaiah 11:6 used to read, 'The Lion shall lie down with the lamb and the bear shall eat grass like the ox. A little child shall play upon the hole of the asp and nothing shall hurt nor destroy in my Holy Mountain.' This passage now reads, 'The *wolf* also shall dwell with the lamb and the leopard shall lay down with the kid and the calf and the young lion and the fatling together: and a little child shall lead them.' The lion represents Christ as the 'Lion of the tribe of Judah' while the wolf has no majestic qualities and is represented in scripture as a devious creature that tries to destroy the sheep. I, personally, know it's altered because as a young Christian I had a poster on my wall showing a lion and lamb, together, with this very verse quoted underneath.

Sand replaced by earth. Luke 6:48-49. A popular song that used to be sung at Sunday school was about the wise man who built his house upon the rock, while the foolish man built his house upon the sand, which subsequently collapsed. This verse now reads, 'But he that heareth and doeth not is like a man that without a foundation built an house upon the *earth* against which the stream did beat vehemently and immediately it fell: and the ruin of the house was great.'

The Jews celebrating Easter not the Passover! Acts 12:4, 'And when he (King Herod) had apprehended him (Peter) he put him in prison and delivered to four quaternion's of soldiers to keep him; intending after *Easter*, to bring him forth to the people.

The false Prophet Ba'-laam provides Ba'-lak with some free advertising! Numbers 24:14, 'And now behold I go unto my people: come therefore, and I will *advertise* thee what this people shall do to thy people in the latter days. The word should be advise not advertise!

Jeremiah 24:2, Vision of the naughty figs. 'One basket had very good figs, even like the figs that are first ripe: and the other basket had *very naughty figs*, which could not be eaten, they were so bad.'

Ezekiel 24:23. Turbans replaced by tires - 'And your *tires* shall be upon your heads, and your shoes upon your feet: ye shall not mourn nor weep; but ye shall pine away for your iniquities, and mourn one toward another.'

If you require further evidence, do an online word search on the words 'corn' and 'bottles' in the Bible Hub online. The first part of the Bible passage is written in a blue coloured font, which has somehow protected it from these changes, while the remaining passage is in a black font. I have put the blue font wording in italics.

Leviticus 2:4 '*If you bring a grain offering of the first-fruits of the Lord, thou shalt offer for the meat offering* of the first-fruits **green ears of corn** dried by the fire, even **corn** beaten out of full ears.'

Psalm 4:7 '*You have filled my heart with more joy than when grain and new wine abound.* Thou hast put gladness in my heart more than in the time that their **corn** and wine increased.'

Deuteronomy 23:25 *'When you enter your neighbour's grain field...*
you may pluck the heads of grain with your hands. When you comest
into the standing **corn** of thy neighbour you mayest pluck the
ears with your hand.'

There are 165 Bible references that have changed grain to
corn and there is another problem. Corn is a 'New World' crop
that was originally found in Mexico. It didn't exist in Israel
at the time of Christ or arrive in the Middle East until the
fifteenth century.

See https://answers.com/Q/Was corn in ancient Middle East

Wineskins changed to bottles. The word wineskins has been
removed and changed to bottles <u>throughout the whole of the</u>
<u>Authorised Version</u>. Matthew 8:17; 'Neither do men put new
wine into old **bottles,** else the **bottles** break, and the wine
runneth out, and the **bottles** perish: but they put new wine into
new **bottles** and both are preserved.' This parable of Jesus no
longer makes any sense, as wineskins may split during the
fermentation process but bottles won't break.

Habakkuk 2:15; *'Woe to him who gives wine to his neighbours,*
pouring it from the wineskin. Woe to him who gives drink to his
neighbour pressing him to your **bottle**.'

When Nabel's wife Abigail, a very astute woman, went out to
meet David and his army, instead of two wineskins containing
gallons of wine, she apparently only took out two bottles giving
them less than a swig each!

1 Samuel 25:18; 'Then Abigail made haste and took two hundred
loaves and two **bottles** of wine and five sheep ready dressed and
five measures of parched **corn**.'

The book of Job, one the most ancient books in the Bible, also mentions being poured out as a bottle before bottles were even invented!

We are therefore left with five different alternatives to explain this phenomenon:

1) The highly intelligent and gifted Bible translators, the leading lights of their day, who originally translated God's word into English made a series of 'school boy' errors when translating the Bible into English from Hebrew and Greek, which are only now coming to light.

2) We have false memory recall when we are remembering what the passages of scripture used to say.

3) The world is under some form of mass hypnosis or psychosis, as people cannot see the words of scripture in the way they are really written so that people lose confidence in the precious Word of God.

4) Time which was once fixed before the Higgs Boson particles were smashed together at CERN, has now become unglued or fluid allowing two, or more, different realities to co-exist and merge together at the same time.

5) According to String Theory at the most microscopic level everything is made out of loops of vibrating strings and apparent particle differences can be attributed to different variations of vibration. Everything can be broken down into atoms, which can then be broken down into electrons and quarks. Finally, these can be broken down into vibrating loops of energy or strings. Some Scientists also believe that ten different dimensions govern our Universe. The fourth dimension is time; while the fifth and sixth are dimensional worlds, only slightly different to our own. Could the constant bombardment of particles near the speed of light have had the unforeseen consequence of somehow opening portals to

a near identical parallel reality that is only slightly different to our own?

https://scienceversesreligion.com/science-vs-god-the-concepts-of-string-theory/

Could these changes to scripture be what the prophet Amos was alluding to when he spoke about the future removal of the word of God from the earth?

Amos 8:11-12: 'Behold, the days come, saith the Lord, that I will send a famine in the land, not a famine of bread nor of thirst of water, but of hearing the words of the Lord and they shall wander from sea to sea, even to the east, they shall run to and fro to seek the word of the Lord and shall not find it.'

Perhaps another way of understanding time, is this - try to think of a giant hour glass full of sand. Each grain of sand represents an hour dating back to the creation of the world. The hour glass is turned over. To the casual observer, as the sand starts to travel downwards, nothing much seems to change in its speed. However, when the amount of sand in the top part of the hour glass has depleted and the downward pressure of time on the sand has reduced, it appears that the final grains of sand seem to dramatically accelerate. God has allocated a certain amount of time for events to play out in this world, and the time he has provided for humanity to repent of its sins, is nearly at an end.

Let's speak plainly here. We can deny that strange events beyond our human understanding are taking place, or we can accept it and realise that this is another sign pointing to the soon return of Jesus Christ to the earth. Satan and his fallen angels have super intelligence and were also known as the 'Sons of God.' Just as Azazel and his fallen host of angels came down to earth and passed occult secrets onto humanity at the time of the Tower of Babel, and the Vril channelled technical details from

'Aliens' providing the Nazis with advanced weaponry, so Satan, who Jesus called the 'Prince of the power of the air,' is passing hidden information to CERN scientists, which will have catastrophic consequences for the earth. There can be little doubt that the Hadron Collider is changing or distorting time as we currently understand it, and opening portals to new forbidden realms, which must now include the potential for some people to travel back in time.

After waiting three years, scientists have again dramatically increased the speed and power of the Hadron Collider's particle smashing capacity.[77] After the removal of the Church from the earth, rather than opening the door to new discoveries, CERN will instead open the portal that contains demonic locust hybrids, that torment all those who have taken Satan's mark, and only after five months will they be able to reverse the Hadron Collider's polarity, and close the inter-dimensional door they opened.

> For the believer it is, 'through faith, we understand that the worlds came into being, and still exist, at the command of God, so that what is seen does not owe its existence to that which is visible.' Hebrews 11:3, Weymouth New Testament.

> The Incomparable Christ- For He has rescued us and has drawn us to Himself from the dominion of darkness, and has transferred us to the kingdom of His beloved Son, in whom we have redemption (because of His sacrifice, resulting in) the forgiveness of our sins (and the cancellation of sin's penalty). He is the exact living image (the essential manifestation) of the unseen God (the visible representation of the invisible), the firstborn (the preeminent one, the sovereign, the originator) of all creation. 'For by Him all things were created in Heaven and on Earth (things) visible

and invisible, whether thrones or dominions or rulers or authorities; all things were created and exist through Him (that is by his activity) and for Him. And He Himself existed and is before all things <u>and in Him all things hold together. (His is the controlling cohesive force of the universe.)</u> Colossians 1:13-17, Amplified Bible

Chapter 13

Type and Anti-Type, History Repeating Itself

In Revelation 13, two beasts are introduced - the beast from the sea and the beast from the earth. Most Bible commentators agree that the beast from the sea represents the Antichrist, who heads up a political force, while the beast from the earth represents a religious system run by the false prophet that will emerge in the last days. Both of these 'beasts' will have their part to play in the control and enslavement of those left behind after the removal of the true church.

However, we then see two references to a third beast being released from the bottomless pit, and returning to the earth. 'When they, (Elijah and Enoch) have finished their testimony, the beast that ascends out of the bottomless pit will make war against them, overcome them, and kill them.' Revelation 11:7, NKJV.

'The beast you saw was once alive but isn't now. And yet he will soon come up out of the bottomless pit and go to eternal destruction and the people who belong to this world, whose names were not written in the Book of Life before the world was made, will be amazed at the re-appearance of the beast who had died.' Revelation 17:8.

The Abomination of Desolation - Matthew 25:14-22

In 168 BC, a message was delivered to Antiochus Epiphanies, a Greek King with a fearsome reputation, when he was advancing against Egypt.[78] The message was from the Roman Senate and was given to Epiphanies by an old Roman official, named Pompilleus Laenus. The message demanded that Epiphanies halted his attack on Egypt as it was a Roman protectorate. He said that he would have to consult with his advisors first. Pompilleus drew a line in the sand around Epiphanies' feet, saying that before he left the circle he would have to give an answer, or consider himself at war with Rome. Antiochus realised that he did not have the resources to attack Rome and complied with Pompilleus's demands, but in so doing lost face in front of his men. In a rage he returned to Palestine and reeked vengeance upon the Jewish community, murdering thousands of men, women and children, without mercy. In verse 15, Jesus made a reference to an historic event that was mentioned by the prophet Daniel. In Daniel 9:27, he mentioned something called 'The Abomination of Desolation,' which took place in 167 BC. Christ's followers would understand that he was referring to Antiochus Epiphanies' sacrilege of the Jewish Temple after Epiphanies had failed to forcibly Hellenise the Jews. He plundered the Jewish temple placing a statue of Zeus there and slaughtered a pig on its altar. He then demanded that the Jews paid homage to the image. He caused the temple sacrifices to cease and anyone who was found with any religious scripts, or each parent who had allowed their sons to be circumcised, were crucified. The Jews referred to Antiochus as Epimanes, which means 'the mad.' Most Bible commentators recognise 'The Little Horn' as mentioned in The Book of Daniel as Antiochus Epiphanies.

The persecution of the Jews was so intense that it led to an armed insurrection by Judas Maccabees. Jesus was informing his followers that the same historic event would repeat itself again during the reign of the Antichrist. He will also place his own image in the temple, cause the Jewish sacrifices to cease and demand to be worshipped as God. Anyone not worshipping him and refusing to receive his mark will be beheaded.

The Hadron Collider is already opening portals to the underworld that God in his wisdom has kept from us. Although the Bible does not specify who this third beast is, it seems highly likely that when the last portal that protects humanity is breached, an angel from God will, I believe, release the imprisoned spirit of Antiochus Epiphanies. He will then return to Earth to possess the body of the Antichrist after he receives a deadly wound and is pronounced dead. The Jew's worst nightmare returns to Earth and continues where he left off. Just as Jesus Christ rose from the dead to give us the hope of eternal life, the book of Revelation reveals to us that someone else will also return from the dead and literally set the world alight and on a pathway to its complete destruction.

Ten facts about the beast from the bottomless pit:

1) He has a Narcissistic Psychopathy in believing that he is God.
2) He had previously existed and died before John wrote the book of Revelation.
3) Only Daniel uses the term 'saints' in the Old Testament and this always refers to New Testament believers and yet we see The Little Horn reappearing to persecute the tribulation saints, just before Christ's return. Daniel 7:21-22, KJV 'I beheld, and the same horn (as persecuted the Jews previously), made war with the saints and prevailed against them. Until the Ancient of Days came and judgement was given to the saints of the most High, and the time came that the saints possessed the kingdom'.
4) One of God's angels will open the bottomless pit half way through the tribulation period, and release the bound

spirit of a 'beast' that had previously died. This would also be about half way through the Antichrist's reign. Revelation 9:1

5) He will return to Earth and the spirit of Epiphanies will possess the dead body of the Antichrist, with Satan being allowed to 'resurrect' him, causing the world to be amazed. Revelation 13:14

6) Unlike the 'first Antichrist', he will be able to kill the two witnesses, Enoch and Elijah, for which he would have to take on human form and not remain as a disembodied spirit. This is after they bring God's judgements to the earth and finish their three and a half year testimony.

7) After three days of lying in the streets of Jerusalem, God will resurrect Elijah and Enoch and they will stand up and then ascend into Heaven and provide evidence of God's true resurrection power, causing great fear and wonder amongst the world's population.

8) He will stop the daily red heifer sacrifices in the temple and declare himself as God.

9) The Antichrist will set up something that represents his own image in the temple (perhaps a hologram or A.I. controlled Avatar) and demand that it is worshipped. The false prophet in charge of the Catholic/Babylonian cult will operate the image and insist people bow down to it.

10) The Antichrist now murders the Catholic/Babylonian priests and destroys the false religious system. Severe persecution of the Jews commences with thousands fleeing Jerusalem to escape being slaughtered, repeating the historical genocide of the Jews caused at Epiphanies' first appearance. Revelation 17:16-18. Matthew 24:15-22.

The invention of the Hadron Collider and the opening of portals to the underworld, will therefore play its part in the fulfilment of biblical prophecy.

Chapter 14

The Trans-human Agenda

To understand why God can no longer 'rest on his laurels' and must shortly intervene by bringing this world to an abrupt end, we need to understand the value that God places on each individual life. The Bible tells us that we are wonderfully and fearfully made. (Psalm 139:14) Human beings are 'God breathed,' which makes us different from the animal kingdom (Genesis 2:51).We are not just another species that has evolved over time. We have a unique place in God's plans and purposes. Once an individual asks Christ into his life, he becomes a born again, new spiritual creation (John 3:3-7).The spiritual communion that was lost in the Garden of Eden through Adam's sin, is instantly restored. The old way of life has gone, the new has come (2 Corinthians 5:17).

Throughout human history, we see repeated efforts to tamper with the unique code that God has placed within all humans, animals and insects. It started with Nimrod's Kingdom and the misgeneration or cross fertilisation of humans with animals. We then see the corruption of mankind's genetic code from the angelic watchers' intermarriage with the daughters of Eve and the birth of the Nephelim (Genesis 6:4).The horrific experiments conducted by Josef Mengele on twins in Auschwitz are shocking examples of what happens when twisted individuals under the control of demonic entities, try to manufacture a master race and eradicate those who these dictators consider 'genetically deficient'.

The Bible reveals that hybrid races roamed the earth in the past and caused havoc. The Nephelim giants caused the children of

Israel to quake and fear when God told them to press forward and inherit the Promised Land. They called themselves grasshoppers when in comparison to the giant races! (Numbers 13:33)This caused them to spend forty years wandering in the wilderness (Numbers 13:34). King Og of Bashan, an Old Testament giant, had a huge bedstead measuring thirteen feet long by six feet wide (Deuteronomy 3:11). Instead of obeying God's commands to completely wipe out Agag the king of the Amalekites, and his animals, King Saul kept hold of hybridised sheep to offer to the Lord as a sacrifice, not a lamb without spot or blemish, as demanded by Levitical Law (Leviticus 3:1). This ultimately caused Saul to be rejected as king (1 Samuel 14: 14-15). However, after these mutated humans were eventually wiped out by King David and his army, God's mercy was shown again towards humanity, including children and animals. God sent his prophet Jonah to Nineveh, a nation that Jonah despised, telling them to repent, which they did, and God's judgement was averted (Jonah 3:10). When God saw what they did, how they turned from their evil ways, God changed his mind about the calamity that he had said he would bring upon them, and he did not do it. But this was very displeasing to Jonah, and he became angry. God told him, 'Should I not be concerned about Nineveh, that great city, in which there are one hundred and twenty thousand people who do not know their right hand from their left, and also many animals?' (Jonah 4:11)

Hitler and Mengele could have only dreamed of the technology that is available today to manipulate our genetic code. A new genetically 'pure' master race is evolving where Crispr[82] will remove any defects or impediments in a pre-born child, and the growing infant can look forward to a menu of genetic modifications as it reaches its teen years. A time of eugenic transformation has arrived, which will bring in a new era, leading again to the hybridization of man's unique genetic code, so that the next generation will no longer be 'fully human.' This attempt to completely wipe out God's original blueprint for our world reveals Satan's 'God envy' and the jealousy he has for the human race. We still have the right through Christ to live in harmony with our Creator and to be lifted to heaven on the wings of angels when we die, and to live in a state of eternal bliss in his presence for evermore.

If Satan can change our God given genetic code so that we are no longer fully human, then we cannot be saved. The Antichrist, interestingly called 'The Beast' in the book of Revelation, will cause the mark they receive to include some sort of genetic material that will make his followers trans-human chimeras and therefore unable to receive salvation.[83] Meanwhile, the devil's fate is already sealed. He will be thrown into the lake of fire and spend eternity in torment with his fallen angels, the Antichrist and all those who died in their sins or accepted his mark.

According to David Estulin, 'What's coming over the next five to ten years will forever revolutionize the very definition of humanity. I can tell you without a doubt that the generations who are being born right now, are the last truly 100% human generation of human beings on the planet. Their children will be trans-human children, post-human, man-machines, cyborgs and beings that are not totally human as a result of synthetic biology. It's absolutely inevitable - the whole idea of merging man and machines.'[84]

This agenda of mankind becoming enhanced, is being promoted to this generation with Marvel comics and films. Almost every hero has some sort of superpowers or uses witchcraft to fight 'evil.' Children are being given the opportunity to transgender. Cars are now hybrids or crossovers. Scientists are experimenting with mixing human, animal and insect

DNA, and the ethical reasons for not proceeding with these Frankenstein experiments are not being heard, nor are the longer term consequences being considered. Pandora's Box is well and truly open and there isn't even much hope left!

Chapter 15

The Dark History of Bill Gates

Since the microchip was invented and patented in 1959 by Jack Kilby and Robert Noyce, mankind has experienced phenomenal technological change and challenges to the way we incorporate information into our everyday lives. The knowledge-doubling curve created by Buckminster Fuller, shows just how fast knowledge is increasing. Up to the year 1900, knowledge doubled every century. By 1945 knowledge doubled every 25 years. After the invention of the microchip, by 1982 knowledge was doubling every 12-13 months. Recently, it was doubling every 72 hours. IBM now estimates that even this will soon change again, to every 12 hours.[85] Very soon, in the time you take to get to work, that is if you can still find a train running, and the time you get home, the totality of human knowledge would have doubled!

This knowledge has allowed technology to rapidly advance and change the way we order our food, the way we meet people, the way we hire a taxi and the way we bank. This has also led to the invention of the 'gig' economy and electronic serfdom. However, this new way of working has also placed an enormous amount of stress onto the workforce, and power into the hands of a few ruthless operators who treat their staff like worker drones.

The myth of how a young Bill Gates, the 'geek-maestro,' founded Microsoft is well known but less known is his family's past ties to the Planned Parenthood Movement.[86] In one interview, Bill claimed his father was the president of the organisation. The roots of the Planned Parenthood clinics began in poorer neighbourhoods like Brooklyn, New York where the first birth control centre opened its doors in the early 1920's.[87]

The birth control movement in America was started by the notorious eugenicist and racist, Margaret Sanger, who was concerned that the 'wrong people' were breeding too quickly and wanted to dramatically reduce the black, Latino and indigenous populations. Sanger was an author of a number of controversial publications and pamphlets, and attempted to gain favour with the numerous eugenics movements that were becoming influential at this time.[89] In 1929, Sanger gave a speech to the Women's Auxiliary Branch of the Ku Klux Klan in Silver Lake, New York City, where she espoused her ideas and thereby, inadvisably, aligned herself to the white supremacist movement and lost personal credibility in the process.[88] In her book 'Women and the New Race,' chapter 5, Sanger wrote about the 'wickedness' of creating large families and advocated infanticide.[89] 'The most merciful thing that a large family does to one of its infant members is to kill it.' In a letter to Dr Clarence J Gamble, Sanger[90] admitted that there was a hidden agenda taking place. She wrote, 'We don't want word to go out that we want to exterminate the Negro population.'

As the writings of Margaret Sanger and the aims and objectives of Planned Parenthood had influenced Bill Gates Senior, so in the 1960's the books authored by Ayn Rand were also having an equal influence on Bill Gates, and the emerging 'Silicon Valley' set of 'microchip technocrats.' Ayn Rand promoted the idea of Objectivism,[91] and that personal fulfilment was the highest aim of man, and saw the church and governments as a barrier to humanity obtaining its full potential. She also viewed altruism as evil. In her books 'Atlas Shrugged' and 'Fountainhead,' Rand's heroes are those who defy convention and push their own selfish personal ideologies regardless of the effects on others. This was just as technocrats were beginning to realise that through the 'microchip revolution,' Governments could be transcended and a new world technocracy installed. The followers of Rand were called Randians and met with her regularly to discuss issues raised in her books. One follower of Rand was Alan Greenspan who became the leader of the Federal Reserve, and he reduced payments to benefit claimants.[92]

The controlling practices of the Bill and Melinda Gates Foundation on the world of medicine, is significant. They part own Pfizer & BioNTech and other Pharma Companies.[93] Money buys influence, and in 2010 a Gates' funded NGO conducted trials of an experimental vaccine in India, without parental permission or explanation of the risks involved. These caused serious vaccine injury and death in a number of children.[94] A parliamentary committee that investigated the case presented a large dossier of evidence to support the claim and concluded that the Foundation had committed 'egregious child abuse.'[95] Not only are the Bill and Melinda Gates Foundation working in partnership with the World Health Organisation, they also worked with the National Aboriginal and Islands Children's Day Organisation (N.A.I.C.D.), and are also developing a digital children's Tattoo alongside The Massachusetts Institute of Technology (MIT) that works using luciferase.[96] A patch containing a number of micro-needles transfers a series of small glowing dots to the hand that can be observed through a photometer or a specially developed app. The Foundation has also financially contributed to the Lucis Trust, previously called The Lucifer Trust.[97]

The UK's Pirbright Institute is also part funded by the Welcome Trust and the Bill and Melinda Gates Foundation and the EU. In November 2018, they registered a coronavirus patent in the US, Patent No 10,130701 B2.

Abstract: The present invention provides a live attenuated corona virus comprising a variant replicase gene encoding polyproteins comprising a mutation in one or more of non structural proteins...*the corona virus may be used as a vaccine* (italics mine) for treating, and, or preventing a disease such as infectious bronchitis in a subject. On page 37 of the patent it states, 'A variant/mutant sequence may arise naturally or be created artificially (for example by site directed mutagenesis). The mutant may have at least 70, 80, 90, 95, 98 or 99% sequence identity with the corresponding portion of the wild type sequence. Could the Omnicron and Monkey Pox virus be just one of several variants that have so quickly mutated from the original coronavirus, as it already had a 'built in' mutation?

The Globalists believe they are so in control that they do little to hide their true intentions. An example of this was Event 201, a Pandemic preparation exercise, which took place in October 2020.[98] This was just a few weeks before the first coronavirus cases started being reported in Wuhan. Each delegate at the event could purchase a cuddly plush coronavirus toy! Attendees included representatives from The Bill and Melinda Gates Foundation, John Hopkins Clinics and the World Economic Forum. 'Live stream' newscasts reported how the predicted virus was spreading throughout the world, and that governments were taking steps to isolate the infected. Transportation systems were being curtailed and flights cancelled. The timing of this event, just before the first major outbreak occurred, would appear to be extremely fortuitous. You may even be led to conclude that the whole thing was planned!

It's hard not to also speculate that Bill Gates' true intentions are to infect the entire world, and then vaccinate it with substances that will start to cause a genetic change in mankind's DNA. The vaccines are a precursor to the mark of the beast system, outlined in Revelation 13:16.

'Also he causes all, both small and great, both rich and poor, both free and slave, to be marked on the right hand or the forehead, so that no one can buy or sell who does not have the mark, that is, the name of the beast or the number of his name. This calls for wisdom: let anyone with understanding calculate the number of the beast, for it is the number of a person. Its number is six hundred and sixty-six (666).'

Our foreheads are meant for the seal of God not Satan's ownership. After the removal of Christians from the earth which is often called the rapture, the Jews will be grafted back in to complete the evangelisation of the world and 144,000 Jewish evangelists are sealed for God's special work and witness. However, just before they start their ministry, and God's judgements commence an angel is told, 'do not damage the earth or the sea or the trees until we have marked the servants of our God with a seal on their foreheads (Revelation 7:3). This mark provides a level of protection against these judgements, just as the children of Israel found protection against the plagues of Egypt by placing the blood of a lamb on their doorposts. However, this will not prevent the eventual martyrdom of the Tribulation Saints.

Although Satan cannot create anything good, he seeks to find people he can manipulate, and then replicate what God is doing, and market it to fallen humanity as an alternative. Just as John the Baptist prepared the way for Jesus Christ's ministry, so Bill Gates is preparing the way for the soon appearance of the Antichrist.

Microsoft's patent ID 2020060606 provides further evidence of this:

Crypto-currency System Using Body Activity.

Abstract: 'Human body activity associated with a task provided to a user may be used in a mining process of a crypto-currency system. A server may provide a task to a device of a user, which is communicatively coupled to the server. The crypto-currency system communicatively coupled to the device of the user may verify if the body activity data satisfies one or more conditions set by the crypto-currency system and award crypto-currency to the user where body activity data is verified.'

This system will reduce mankind to the level of performing chimps. What is not made clear by the patent is if the 'communication device' stated is wearable or placed under the skin. So why is there such a rush to implement this micro-chip system? Do the Elite know something we don't?

Hitlers 'UFO' The Vril inspired Haunebu 2 being loaded

Coming to America. The Operation Paperclip
rocket scientists at Fort Bliss, Texas 1946

Nazi Hunter Simon Wiesenthal

Adolf Eichmann on trial in Jerusalem

The Stanley Milgram electric shock machine

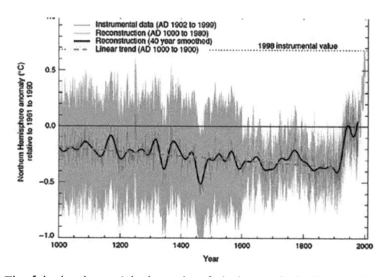

The fake hockey-stick chart that failed to include the medieval warm period and the little ice age shown below

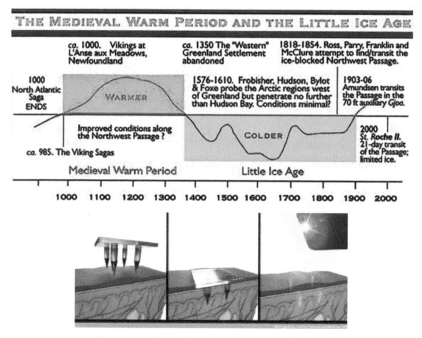

Quantum Dot Tatoos Using Luciferase
For Track And Trace Purposes

FAA webcams show a rapidly rotating Orb caught in earth's orbit

10 minutes later. Notice the changing lens flare on the lower right

The Geoengineering nightmare continues.
Chemtrails over Malvern

107
total known
near-Earth comets

20,141
total known
near-Earth asteroids

896
total known NEOs
larger than 1,000m

20,248
total known
near-Earth objects

8,609
total known NEOs
larger than 140m

PLANETARY
SOCIETY

There has been a huge increase in dangerous Near Earth
Objects and asteroids located close to the earth

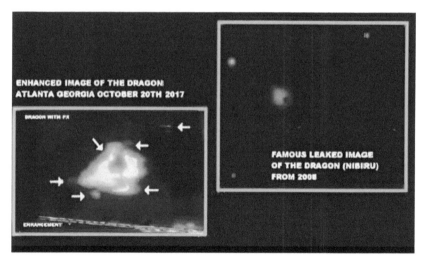

ENHANCED IMAGE OF THE DRAGON
ATLANTA GEORGIA OCTOBER 20TH 2017

DRAGON WITH FX

ENHANCEMENT

FAMOUS LEAKED IMAGE
OF THE DRAGON (NIBIRU)
FROM 2008

Leaked pictures of Nibiru 'Planet X' aproaching earth

Denver Airport with Apocalyptic murals

Nazi Alien with sabre Kills the dove of peace

The Vatican's Infrared Telescope on Mount Graham

In Vatican City Cherub's pay homage to the Nazi Black Eagle

Snake charmer at the Vatican. The Pope's
seat is set between the serpents fangs

The resurrected 'reptilian' Christ with the head of a serpent

The Pope shares a message in front of this
disturbing Gothic backdrop

Carving of Babylonian King Nimrod with Pine Cone.

In Vatican City-The pine cone represents the
opening of the Illuminated third eye

Another huge sink hole not mentioned on the news

Continental shift in Africa. Land masses are
beginning to pull themselves apart

A plush Coronavirus toy could be purchased at Event 201

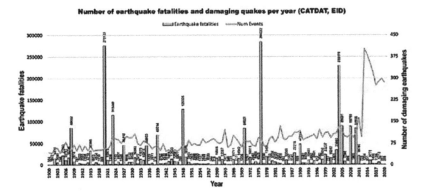

There has been a dramatic uptick in earthquakes since 2012

CERN and its interlocking 666 logo

TABLE 19

| IFN-alpha signal | | | | |
| IFN-alpha signal - 2 donor average | | | | |

pg/mL	2 Hr	4 Hr	8 Hr	20 Hr	44 Hr
G-CSF (5mC/pseudouridine)	21.1	2.9	3.7	22.7	4.3
G-CSF (5mC/N1-methyl pseudouridine)	0.5	0.4	3.0	2.3	2.1
G-CSF (Natural)	0.0	2.1	23.3	74.9	119.7
Luciferase (5mC/pseudouridine)	0.4	0.4	4.7	1.0	2.4
R-848	39.1	151.3	278.4	362.2	208.1
Lipofectamine 2000 control	0.8	17.2	16.5	0.7	3.1

Experiments to increase the bioluminesense of Luciferase as seen on the Moderna Website

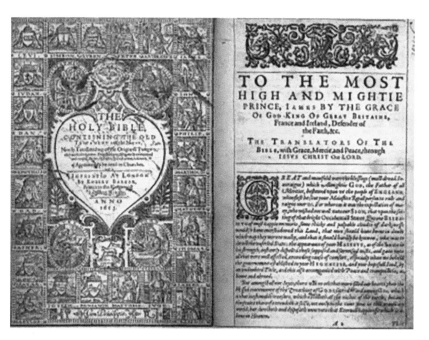

Even the earliest printed Bibles now state 'Prince' James

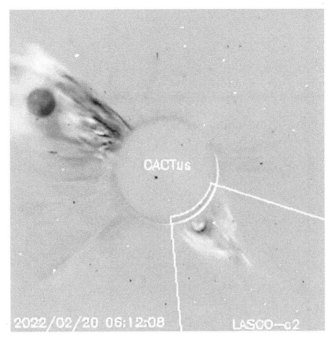

Nibiru at 10 o'clock and a companion planet at 5 o'clock causing huge Coronal Mass Ejections. As seen by the Soho satellite

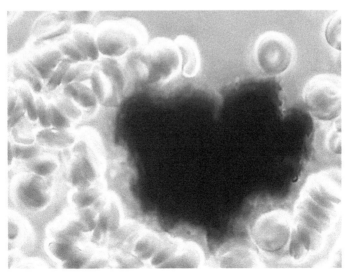

Graphine Oxide reacting to human blood cells

Located at CERN Geneva. Shiva starts the dance of destruction

The World Economic Forum wants you
to own nothing and be happy

Chapter 16

Countdown to Catastrophe

Did you realise that 80% of the stars in our Universe have a 'binary twin?'[99] According to the Chilean astronomer, Munos Ferrada, we have a black sun companion to our sun, which Nibiru (Planet X), circulates and then returns back to *our* sun, about every 3,600 years in an elliptical orbit.[100] This is most likely a red or a brown Dwarf Star which has a failing light source in a distant part of our undiscovered solar system. If this is the case, Nibiru's last passing would have had a direct influence on the earth and could have caused Noah's flood. Jesus told us that the last days on earth would resemble those at the time of Noah. It is possible that Christ's words also indicate that the real cause of Noah's flood, (Planet X), will again return to create chaos upon the earth at the end of this current age. The ancient Samarians showed Nibiru as a shining star with two wings on their hieroglyphics at its last passing.[101]

In 1977, NASA launched its two Voyager satellites containing infrared equipment as the planets had lined up in a certain way, which would allow them to use the gravitational pull of Jupiter, Saturn, Uranus and Neptune to propel the Voyagers forward. At that time NASA made no secret that they were trying to find a new planet, which would be the tenth, or X in Roman numerals: sometimes called Nibiru − the passing planet.[102] That is, until NASA changed Pluto's designation from a planet to a 'dwarf planet.'

NASA had observed a perturbation in the orbits of Uranus and Neptune, but could not understand what was causing this unusual movement, and could not, at that time, observe or view any mysterious planetary bodies even through their largest telescopes. Scientists were so convinced that Planet X existed and that it might be inhabited that they placed two golden phonograph records on each satellite with 'Sounds of the Earth' and a diagram showing earth's location in our solar system.[103] This was after the Pioneer 10 satellite launched in 1972 had discovered an object in the far reaches of our solar system, using its onboard infrared radiometer imaging equipment. NASA, growing increasingly concerned about what influence this mystery object would have on the earth, launched yet another satellite in 1983. The IRAS Infrared satellite had a ten month mission to rotate at 360 degrees and take panoramic photographs of the Universe.[104] This would confirm what NASA feared the most, that the perturbation between Uranus and Neptune **was** being triggered by a massive planetary body that can only be observed within the infrared spectrum, and which has an enormous gravitational pull.

Realising that Nibiru would cause a series of catastrophic world events, the Elite would use every tool at their disposal to deceive and hide this information from the general public. What has transpired is a worldwide disinformation and depopulation programme, as our media and news outlets actively promote the 'man-made' global warming myth from the Intergovernmental Panel on Climate Change.

Observations by Mike Brown and Konstantin Batygin, who work for the California Institute of Technology, have discovered the effects of what is now being called Planet 9.[105] Brown believes that at one time, Pluto could have been one of Neptune's moons which was disrupted and pulled out of orbit at one of Planet 9's previous appearances. Batygin stated that its orbit is perpendicular and it travels further than 20 Astronomical Units beyond our solar system and then returns.[106] Brown believes that Planet 9's gravitational effects are so great that it is tilting our solar system at an angle of six degrees. As Nibiru passed through the Oort Cloud[107] and near the Kuiper Belt, it has picked up a huge amount of debris consisting of rocks and space dust. According to the book of Revelation, during the seven year tribulation period, the earth will be pelted and pummelled with a huge amount of space rocks, with some rocks weighing over 100 pounds.

Chapter 17

Evidence that the Earth is being affected by an External Force

1 The Written Word

Although NASA, (Never A Straight Answer) continues to deny the existence of Planet X and labels its adherents as 'conspiracy theorists,' it's hard for them to argue with their own findings as they were the first ones to announce the planet's discovery in the first place, and have since tried to airbrush away all the evidence. However, newspaper articles from 1983 still exist today. In an article written for The Washington Post, underscored 'Democracy Dies In Darkness,' written by Thomas O'Toole on December 30ᵗʰ 1983, and titled 'Possibly as large as Jupiter.' The article went on to explain about the most recent discovery of a huge object in space that has the Jet Propulsion Labs buzzing with excitement. The heavenly body was found to be so close to earth that it could be part of our solar system, and had been found by an orbiting telescope aboard the IRAS, Infrared Astronomical Satellite.

Dr Gerry Neugebauer, IRAS chief scientist for California's Jet Propulsion Laboratory stated, 'The most fascinating explanation of this mystery body which is so cold that it casts no light and has never been seen by optical telescopes in earth or in space, as it is a giant gaseous planet the size of Jupiter and as close to Earth as 50 billion miles. While that might seem like a great distance in earthbound terms, it is a stone's throw in cosmological terms, so close in fact that it would be the nearest heavenly body to Earth beyond the outermost planet Pluto. The mystery body was seen twice by the Infrared Satellite as it scanned the northern sky from last January to November (1983) when the satellite ran out of the super-cold helium that allowed the telescope to see the coldest bodies in the heavens.'

Dr James Houck of Cornell University's Centre for Radar Physics and Space Research, and a member of the IRAS Science Team said, 'That if it is really that close it would be part of our solar system.' The team thought that they had discovered a Proto-star, an object that had never got hot enough to become a star.

However, if Planet X or Nibiru poses no threat to our civilisation, why has nearly all debate on its discovery been silenced? A number of those who study this subject believe that our Sun's dark visitor is on a 3,600 year elliptical orbit with a trajectory that will shortly take it past our Sun. As it accelerates to achieve 'breakaway' speed and escape from our solar system, a series of catastrophic events will take place, including the Earth being pelted with a massive amount of space rocks.

2 Climate Change is Happening throughout Our Entire Solar System

If climate change can be shown to be affecting not only our own planet but also other planets within our solar system, then the whole climate change agenda, which is based on 'man-made' CO_2 being the main driver of environmental change, is false, and we have entered a completely new 'cause and effect' paradox. How could increasing CO_2 on Earth create climate change within the Martian atmosphere? The whole green sustainability road-show, which is making a lot of people very rich, especially in the trading of 'Carbon Credits,' is therefore also bogus as we can do nothing to change the inevitable!

In a ground breaking study released in 1999, Dr Mike Lockwood,[107] who worked for Rutherford Appleton National Labs, provided irrefutable evidence that our Sun has been undergoing a number of significant changes during its maunder minimum and maunder maximum eleven year cycles. During a maunder minimum our Sun hibernates and sunspot activity is dramatically reduced while volcanic activity on the earth increases.

Over the last one hundred years there have been notable changes within each Sun cycle and this is having a disruptive influence over all of our eco systems. A 'YouTube' video which highlights Mike's findings was produced in 1999, and provides further evidence that the Sun's magnetic field has increased in intensity by 230% since 1901.[108] The Moon has developed a 6000km atmospheric layer of Natrium. There are now ice caps on the north and south poles of Mercury, which has developed a very strong magnetic field. There have been substantive changes in Venus's atmosphere over the last forty years leading to an increase in its aurora brightness of 2,500%. Mars is experiencing huge storms and the disappearance of its ice caps. Jupiter's plasma clouds have become brighter by 200% and the huge belts in the giant planet's atmosphere have changed colour, and had space rocks pummelling its surface. Saturn has had a major decrease in its equatorial jet stream velocities in the last thirty years and a surprising surge of x-rays coming from the equator. Uranus has had a huge increase in aurora brightness and cloud activity. Neptune has had a 40% increase in aurora brightness. Pluto has had a massive increase in atmospheric density.

Our own Earth has seen shrinking ice caps, increase in sink holes, earthquakes, flooding and volcanic activity; there have been landslides causing disruption and the ground is becoming unstable.

In 2007, an article in 'Live Science' magazine, acknowledged that climate change within our solar system had become a 'hot topic' of conversation within the scientific community.'[109] Benny Peiser, a social anthropologist at Liverpool John Moore's University, stated that 'Global warming on Neptune's moon Triton as well as Jupiter and Pluto and now Mars has some scientists scratching their heads over what could possibly be in common with the warming of all these planets...' He asked the question, 'Could there be something in common with all the planets in our solar system that might cause them all to warm at the same time?'

Habibullo Abdussamatov, the head of space research in St. Petersburg's Pulkova Astronomical Observatory, linked the attenuation of ice caps on Mars to fluctuation in the Sun's output. He also blamed 'solar fluctuations' for Earth's current global warming trends. 'Man-made greenhouse warming has made *a small contribution* (italics mine) to the warming on Earth in recent years, but it cannot compete with the increase of solar irradiance. The heating and cooling on the Earth and Mars always will be practically parallel.' However, others believe that the thawing ice caps on Mars are due to variations to the planets natural orbit and tilt. On Earth, these wobbles are known as the Milankovitch cycles and these 'wobbles' on the Earth and Mars are intensifying.

NASA's Bill Nelson has warned us that in the 2030's there will also be a 'wobble' in the moon's cycle. This happens every 18.6 years and will affect earth's low and high tides. This will have a devastating effect on low-lying areas when they are predicting another surge of severe coastal flooding.[110]

3 Our North and South Magnetic Poles have become Erratic

Scientists are struggling to understand why there are a number of changes happening deep within the Earth's core, which may be the main driver for climate change and the real reason why ice flows are rapidly melting. In an article written for Nature magazine, scientists found deep core 'slushing' taking place,[111] which is causing serious affects to the Earth's magnetic north and south poles while melting Greenland's ice shelf.[112] The range of change by which our navigational models are based were found to be highly inaccurate years before the next proposed change. The rate at which the magnetic north pole is now accelerating year on year, has caused scientists to speculate that the earth may be on the verge of a dramatic pole shift.[113] However, this doesn't mean that they automatically swap positions, north becoming south etc. What is more likely, is that they will both splinter and control different parts of the earth's surface, leading to huge problems with our communication networks.

As a direct consequence of the rapid shift in our magnetic poles, serious consequences are being felt by our sea life. It is only just recently that we have begun to understand how birds and fish utilise the magnetic poles for navigational purposes.[114] As our poles become erratic, whole ecosystems are now under threat. Expect this traumatic situation to become critical over the next few years with far more whale, dolphin and schools of fish becoming beached.

4 Prophesied Global Fires now Occurring

The prophet Esdras was given insight into global conditions just before Christ's return to the Earth. Esdras 5:8 'There will be chaos in many places and fires will break out often.' Although it is not surprising for fires to start in hottest parts of the globe, what is happening today is that fires are breaking out near the Arctic Circle! In August 2017, Greenland's Remote Sensing scientists discovered that a number of fires were occurring in Sisimiut on the Arctic Circle trail. The fires unexpectedly broke out again on July 10th 2019. In June 2022, The National Oceanic Atmospheric Administration (N.O.A.A.), found that in Alaska three hundred wildfires were burning out of control damaging one million acres of Alaska's tundra. During the seven year tribulation period, there will be a huge increase in global temperatures due to God's wrath on unrepentant sinners. 'And the fourth angel poured out his vial upon the Sun and power was given unto him to burn men with fire.' Revelation 16:8 KJV

5 The Vatican's Telescope

The Vatican owns an infrared telescope, which is based at Mount Graham in Arizona. In a 'Coast to Coast' radio interview, conducted by Art Bell with Father Malachi Martin in 1997, Art asked why the Vatican had purposely 'muscled their way' onto Mount Graham to place an observatory there? Malachi replied, 'The attitude, the mentality, amongst those who at the higher level, the highest levels, of Vatican geopolitics know that, now, *knowledge of what's going on in space and what's approaching* (italics mine) could be of great import in the next five to ten years.'[115]

6 The Earth's Surface is already in a State of Collapse

Sinkholes in the ground are usually caused by something called the 'Karst Process.'[116] As water eats away at permeable rocks like gypsum or limestone, a dip or depression appears just before the ground gives way, so areas with little or no exposure to water should not be affected. However, this is now a worldwide phenomenon with sinkholes appearing in places that receive low amounts of annual precipitation, including some of the hottest places on Earth such as Australia and Brazil.

In Kuwait, four cylindrical sinkholes first appeared between April 1988 and June 1989, when the ground around them became unstable in a residential area of Kuwait City. However, this was not a one off event and has become a reoccurring nightmare. The latest sinkholes caused considerable economic problems between 2020 and 2021. Kuwait's annual rainfall is between 3-5mm.

Tectonic plates have always shifted but massive cracks are now appearing on the Earth's surface. In 2018, a deep crack appeared in Kenya near Nairobi measuring hundreds of metres long and over fifteen metres deep.[117] In Mexico City another huge crack appeared, destroying houses and a railway, cutting across a major road and causing part of the city to shift downwards. The whole area around Guatemala became unstable when a number of huge sinkholes and landslides caused serious problems.[118]

7 Going underground

Governments worldwide are all building huge bunker facilities. Since 2015, in the U.S. over three hundred Walmart's and Sam's Clubs have closed across the States, never to re-open.[119] They all simultaneously cited 'plumbing issues' and laid off all their staff. Within a few weeks, the stores were completely cleared of stock and the outside perimeters were turned into mesh covered containment areas. These were then taken over by the Federal Emergency Measures Agency (F.E.M.A).

There are now over eight hundred of these 'Internment Camps' dotted around the United States that can hold up to two thousand 'inmates' each, and a massive facility has been constructed in Fairbanks, Alaska, that can contain over two million citizens. These camps are all interconnected by a network of Deep Underground Military Bases (D.U.M.B.),[120] which are serviced by fast moving mono-rail trains. On September 26th 1972, a patent was granted for 'A method and apparatus for tunnelling by melting.' This US Patent No 3693,731 was given worldwide approval and was purchased by the US Government.

This Thermo-nuclear cutting device heats its drill tip to an astonishing two thousand degrees Fahrenheit, and turns rock particles into glass, which it then uses to seal the sides of the tunnel. In the UK, the HS2 tunnel has been partially completed while massive super prisons have been built in Glen Parva, Leicester[121] and Wellingborough[122]. These facilities will hold thousands of extra prisoners using the 'Lend-Lease' system, something that the government hasn't used since World War 2. Why, during a time of huge financial constraint, has money been allocated to complete such massive projects unless it is viewed by our leaders as an absolute imperative?

8 Space Force, DART and DAMIEN

Space Force was founded in 2019 and initially given a budget of $15.4 billion. This budget has increased to $24.5 billion for the year 2023. Space Force has a staff of over six thousand people and is in control of Space Based Infrared Systems (S.B.I.S.),[123] which are intended to meet the US space surveillance needs through the next two to three decades. These are satellites that contain weaponry and are in a geosynchronous orbit, which means that they rotate around the earth every 23 hours, 54 minutes and 4 seconds and are always kept in the same position. This is the same pathway expected to be used by so called 'exo-planets' and asteroids.

- The successful Double Asteroid Redirection Test (D.A.R.T.) mission that recently deflected the moonlet from asteroid Didymos has caused the moonlet to develop twin tails and change its orbit.[124] This mission is an integral part of the National Near Earth Object Preparedness Strategy, which was itself proposed by the Interagency Working Group for Detecting And Mitigating The Impact of Earth-Bound Near Earth Objects (DAMIEN IWG).[125] In its conclusion their report states, 'Near Earth Objects impacts pose a significant and complex risk to human life and critical infrastructure and have the potential to cause substantial and possibly unparalleled economic and environmental harm.' Anyone familiar with 'The Omen' franchise will recognise that Damien Thorn was the name given to the Antichrist by his parents. Future threats from space and chaos on the ground will provide an opportunity for the Antichrist to seize power and control a One World Government, run by a powerful Elite.

#9 The Inuit's Testimonies

In the revelatory documentary, 'Inuit knowledge and climate change' released on November 25th 2009, and shown on Isuma TV, a multimedia broadcaster for this indigenous population, the highly regarded film producer Zacharius Kanut conducted a series of interviews with the indigenous people who inhabit the regions of the Canadian Arctic, Greenland, Siberia and Alaska. These tribes completely rely on the Sun for survival as it determines how long they can hunt for seals and fish. They state that the seals now have burn marks on their skins and that the Sun, Moon and stars have all changed position. The Sun now rises and sets in different locations than it has in the past, and this has extended their hunting time by two hours a day. They have concluded that greenhouse gases are not causing climate change but that 'THE EARTH'S AXIS HAS SHIFTED AND THE WINDS NO LONGER BLOW IN THE SAME DIRECTION.' The Inuits have a deep understanding of the ways of the Earth and sky and have been hunting and fishing for generations in these inhospitable regions. Mummified tree trunks, covered in deep snow, have also been discovered in these northern zones, providing further evidence of a warmer climate in the past. The Inuits are the 'real' climate experts and we

should believe their testimony because their lives depend completely on the natural environment!

10 Scientific Discoveries by Harrington and Ferrada

The testimonies of Dr. Robert Harrington, supervising astronomer at the US Naval Observatory in Washington DC, and Carlos Munos Ferrada, astronomer and seismologist, who was incredibly accurate in his predictions, both concluded that a huge planetary intruder is lurking within our solar system. According to Ferrada, this would soon be the harbinger of numerous catastrophic world events taking place.

Robert Harrington was involved in both the Pioneer and IRAS missions into deep space. While 'The Grand Tour' took place when the planetary bodies all lined up so that Voyagers 1 and 2 would use the gravity of each of our planets to 'sling-shot' the satellite to the next planet in our solar system. In an interview with Zachariah Sitchen, Dr. Harrington calculated that to cause such perturbation in the orbits of Uranus and Neptune, the mass of the planetary body would have to be at least five times the circumference of the Earth.[126]

Munos Ferrada made a number of startling climatology predictions and is credited with correctly publishing a warning about an earthquake that would take place within a few days in the Chilean 'El Sur' newspaper published on January 19th 1939.[127] He used his own privately developed monitoring equipment and not only stated the date of the earthquake as 24th of January, but also the time. On 24th January, a massive earthquake measuring 9.5 devastated five provinces of southern Chile, killing over 40,000 people and caused widespread damage. Ferrada had not only calculated the correct date for the disaster but there was only two hours difference between the times he predicted the earthquake would start and when it actually occurred.

Due to the incredible accuracy in his calculations and astronomical discoveries, one being that Halley's Comet would change speed and direction at the last moment, which actually took place on February 12th 1996, Ferrada became recognised by the Royal Astronomical Observatory.[128] They also agreed with Ferrada's request that any newly discovered planetary bodies should be named after the person who first calculated it and not the individual who first observed it.

Near the end of his life in a television interview, Ferrada reiterated that Nibiru, which he called Hercolubus, would again pass by the Earth.[129] Showing his charts, he explained to the reporter that the trajectory of Hercolubus takes it past our Sun's distant dark nemesis, the black Sun, then with the dark Sun's gravitational force slingshots it back towards our own Sun. Try to think of a large rubber band with two index fingers at each end representing our Sun and the black Sun with the elastic band representing the planet's elongated orbit. This process takes around 3,600 years. Ferrada called this planetary body the 'comet star' as it is the size of a large planet but it also has all the characteristics of a comet.

By 2009, the effects of climate change were becoming so stark that the costs of aerosol spraying in the UK were actively being considered. A Parliamentary Paper on Geo-engineering and Solar Radiation Management (S.R.M.)[130] was issued that also considered the costs of placing mirrors into space in a low earth orbit to reflect back the Sun's rays. This would cost one trillion dollars. Although not mentioned in this paper, space mirrors could also be used as a cloaking device. As events accelerate us way beyond our Earth's tipping point, the information you have gleaned in this book will give you the knowledge to best prepare for the series of major apocalyptic events that are now on the horizon.

Chapter 18

The Intergovernmental Panel on Climate Change and the Medieval Warm Period

'It is dangerous to be right in matters where established men are wrong' – Voltaire

The 'Medieval Warm Period' is an extreme embarrassment to the climate change lobby as it signifies that we have had previous times of heating and cooling of the planet that has nothing to do with human activity. In 1965, Hubert Horace Lamb a British Climatologist examined the historical records of ice cores and tree ring data. With this information he was able to conclude that in the MWP people experienced balmy temperatures between 1.8 to 3.6 degrees Fahrenheit above the norm.

Professor Deming, in Science Magazine 1995, said, 'I gained significant credibility in the community of scientists working on climate change. They thought I was one of them, someone who would pervert science in the service of social and political causes. So one of them let his guard down. A major person working in the area of climate change and global warming sent me an astonishing e-mail that said, 'We must get rid of the Medieval Warm Period.'

The I.P.C.C. was set up just a few years after the discovery of Nibiru to provide misdirection and a viable alternative to why so many changes on earth are taking place. Governments are using the climate change narrative in an attempt to control our way of life. Meteorologist Klaus-Eckart Puls was so infuriated by the deception being perpetuated by the climate change lobby, that he said;

'Ten years ago I simply parroted what the IPCC told us. One day I started checking the facts and data. First, I started with a sense of doubt but then I became outraged when I discovered that much of what the IPCC and the media are telling us was sheer nonsense, and was not even supported by any scientific facts and measurements. To this day I still feel shame that as a scientist I made presentations of their science without first checking it. The CO_2 climate hysteria in Germany is propagated by people who are in it for lots of money, attention and power.'

It was noted by Joanne Nova that between 1989 and 2009, and using completely unscientific processes, the US Government had spent '$79 billion to fund thousands of scientists to find a connection between human carbon emissions and the climate.'[131] Hardly any have been funded to find the opposite. 'Throw $30 billion dollars at one question and how could bright, dedicated people not find eight hundred pages worth of connections, links, predictions, projections and scenarios? What's amazing is what they haven't found: empirical evidence.'[132]

The Doomsday book, written in 1087, provided the English king with the first real survey of his kingdom. It mentions populations, farms and forty-six vineyards producing top quality wine. These were mainly around Ely in Cambridgeshire and Gloucester, with one located as far north as Derby. It was so warm that the Vikings established a group of settlements on Greenland.[133]

Now look at the subterfuge being deployed by those who seek to use the environment as a tool to control human activity. This included those, who, in 1988, purposely arranged a meeting to discuss climate change with the US Senate Committee on one of the hottest days of the year, and intentionally sabotaged the room's air conditioning system. This provided more 'evidence' on climate change being acknowledged by those who attended the meeting.[134]

'Today's debate about global warming is essentially a debate about freedom. The environmentalists would like to mastermind each and every possible and impossible aspect of our lives.' *Vaclav Klaus - Blue Planet in Green Shackles.*

There is a Hans Christian Anderson tale about an Emperor who adored new clothes and wore a different outfit every day. A couple of confidence tricksters came into town pretending to be tailors. They promised to produce the most exquisite and luxurious garment the Emperor had ever seen. Just one thing they said, only a wise man will see the beautiful garment, but a fool who is unfit for his elected office will not. He set the tailors to work then sent a number of his officials to check on their progress and to see if the people he employed were wise or not. Not wanting to appear fools, or lose their status or positions in the Emperor's Court, the officials all returned with glowing reports about the finery of the clothes they had seen being produced on empty looms. It was a day of great procession and the Emperor decided to wear his new outfit at the parade. The bystanders, who had been warned about this charade, and not wanting to embarrass the Emperor, all agreed what magnificent clothes he was wearing.' It was a small child that had not been pre-conditioned to this farce that cried out, 'The Emperor is naked!'

Now just imagine that this Emperor lived in 1650 at the time period known as 'The Little Ice Age,' which lasted from 1500-1700 when sunspot activity was practically non-existent and winter fairs took place on a frozen River Thames. He is concerned that human activity is to blame for global cooling and hates the extensive bonfires that are being lit; keeping people warm but stinking up his kingdom. He sends for those same compliant courtiers who saw the empty looms and gives them an order. 'Prove to me that human activity is to blame for this big freeze and there is a bag of gold in it for you.'

The Courtiers look at the historic records and realise that between 950 and 1250 AD, there was a period of time when the earth heated up, called, 'The Medieval Warm Period.' To prove their human activity theory, they develop a model that charts the reduction in temperature from the highest part of 'The Warm Period' to the lowest part of 'The Little Ice Age.' They decide to rule out sunspot activity and instead include data on the burning of logs in the fireplace, bonfires and pig roasts. The Courtiers explain to the Emperor that these events have increased dramatically over the last one hundred years, and that the dense smoke in the atmosphere has blocked the sun's rays hitting the Earth, reducing its capacity to warm the planet. The Emperor uses the information he needs so he can present his case to the peasants and get them to agree to reduce the amount of smelly bonfires being lit in his kingdom, and the Courtiers get their reward. In other words, start with the conclusion you desire, and then work your way back to make your research fit around it to achieve the desired result.

The 'prove or disprove' a theory requires something called the' Scientific method.' This is completed in four stages:

- Form a hypothesis - A statement or theory that can be thoroughly tested.
- Make observations - conduct extensive tests and experiments to determine if the theory is correct or not.
- Analyse and interpret the data - test again if necessary.
- Draw conclusions - Is the theory false, true or partly true?

Now let's compare this with the IPCC's non-scientific method:

- Start with the conclusion that manmade CO_2 is causing climate change.
- Limit, filter and exclude any observations that contradict this theory.
- Tweak and manipulate the data so that it fits.
- Create a hypothesis that works in tandem with the conclusion.
- Publish your findings: one report for the press with stark warnings, and another for the science community issued later that looks quite different. This is so, sometime in the future, when the rubber hits the road, and greenhouse gases are proved to have no correlation at all to climate change, you can blame the press for sensationalism.

The release of 10,000 confidential memos from the University of East Anglia in 2009, which became known as 'Climate-gate,'[135] revealed some of the doubts and deception being utilised by climate scientists to 'prove' that man-made CO_2 is the only cause of climate change. Exactly two years to the day that the first 'Climate-gate' emails were released, another 5,000 were leaked on 22nd November 2011. Called Climate-gate 2.0, it revealed the following themes:

1) Prominent scientists central to the global warming debate are taking measures to conceal rather than disseminate underlying data and discussions.
2) These climate scientists view global warming as a 'political' cause rather than a balanced science enquiry.
3) Many of these scientists frankly admit to each other that much of the science is weak and dependent on deliberate manipulation of facts and data.

A report issued by Joseph Dalio, First Director of Meteorology and Co-founder of the Weather Channel, released a report on the dubious alarmist claims that were also found to be false that by 2035 the glaciers on the Himalayas would completely disappear. Dubbed 'Glacier-gate' the report was later to be found to be inaccurate by 350 years![136]

The 'Hockey Stick' chart (See Picture Gallery),[137] produced by Michael Mann published in 2001, presented a sharp rise in global temperatures and was used in a number of publications and science journals. It was eventually proved to be a complete fabrication. It was updated a few years later and presented further 'evidence' that global warming had dramatically increased over the last two decades. However, the 'Hockey Stick' chart, no doubt the subject of academic debates and many a thesis, excluded information on the commonly accepted Medieval Warm Period where temperatures were well above our current levels, and eradicated the cold temperature of the Little Ice Age.

Climate sceptic Tim Ball was so affronted by this data manipulation that he commented that Michael Mann should 'live in State Pen not Penn State.' At this, Mann started litigation proceedings against Ball. Year after year Mann continued to obfuscate, refusing to supply the court with the mathematical equations on which his findings were based. The court finally lost patience and ruled in Ball's favour, granting him court costs and prevented Mann from re-opening the case.[138] Tim has produced an excellent book entitled 'The Deliberate Corruption of Climate Science,' which presents an in-depth expose in an easy-to-read format on all the mendacious machinations in the heart of the climate change empire.

Take for instance the 'Keeling Curve' invented by Charles Keeling.[139] He took meticulous measurements from 1958 and built a graph showing the continuous growth of CO_2 in the atmosphere from that date until 2020. Well of course, no-one doubts that there has been a rise in CO_2 in the atmosphere since the dramatic growth in factory production, car ownership and plane travel, with a small Chemtrail cocktail mix thrown in for good measure. However, this does not prove that the increase in greenhouse gases correlates to all the severe changes taking place on our planet. This is just another theory. How is it possible to conclude that the rise in sinkholes appearing all over the planet, dormant volcanoes becoming active, annual floods, deadly earthquake activity and landslides claiming thousands of lives, are all due to an incremental increase in CO_2 emissions?

For our Globalist manipulators, the corruption of climate science is viewed as the lesser of two evils. The other is to 'go public' and admit that some other force is affecting our solar system, which absolutely no-one will have any control over. So they must, as long as they can, fan the flames of 'man-made' global warming myths, while their more fanatical band of environ-mentalists block roads, climb onto the top of train carriages, let down the tyres of high performance vehicles and try to prevent fuel trucks from leaving their depots.

However, the worshippers of GAIA must keep beating their pagan drums ever louder, to ward off the chorus of ascending voices who believe that the whole thing is just a lot of 'hot air' without substance. The New World Order's Room 101 'Ministry of Fear' will continue to orchestrate a series of climate change shocks, food shortages, pandemics, financial meltdowns, terror outrages, disasters, and wars against terror, drugs and everything else to maintain a continuous worldwide state of anxiety and fear. They want to pre-condition our minds so that we will eventually be willing to give up our human rights in exchange for international security.

Chapter 19

The Pope, The Vatican's Infrared Telescope and the Secretum Omega

Although it is not too unusual for a religious organisation to own a telescope as the stars tell forth the story of God's marvellous creation, what *is* unusual is that the Vatican has built an expensive Infrared Telescope on Mount Graham in the Nevada Desert, which is a sacred place for the resident Indian population.

The Vatican's Advanced Technology Telescope (VATT) is run in partnership with The University of Arizona. Alongside the Vatican's telescope, and sharing the same mountain, is another infrared telescope called, the Large Binocular Telescope (LBT),[140] which uses an instrument that was originally called 'LUCIFER.' It's a convoluted acrostic but stands for The **L**arge binocular telescope near-infrared **U**tility with **C**amera and **I**ntegral **F**ield unit for **E**xtra-Galactic **R**esearch.

Operating the telescope is a consortium that includes The Max Planck Institute for Extraterrestrial Physics.[141] Planck's website states that the Large Binocular Telescope is a collaboration between astronomical institutes in Germany, Italy and the US.

Regular observations started in 2009, and the name of the instrument was changed from LUCIFER to LUCI in 2012. Like all infrared instruments, the LBT and the Vatican's VATT are operated at cryogenic temperatures and enclosed in a cryostat of 1.6m diameter and 1.6m height and cooled down to about -200 degrees by two closed cycle coolers. You may ask why the

Vatican and the Max Planck Institute need two telescopes in such close proximity that reveals things that can't be seen by the naked eye, especially infrared telescopes, unless of course, there is something going on in space that will have a significant impact on all of us.

In the year 2000, the editor of Stargate Magazine, Christoforo Bailato, who had written some articles on the 'third secret' of Fatima, was contacted by a Vatican insider who claimed that he worked for the SIV (Servizio Informazioni del Vaticano - the Pope's Secret Intelligence Service).[142] The SIV consists of about one hundred Jesuits and others who are specialists in their own fields of scientific activity. The insider had liked the article that Christoforo had written and had knowledge that linked the third secret of Fatima with observations that had been obtained from the VATT. Christoforo was then sent a video of these observations, which had shown a huge planetary body approaching Earth taken from the Vatican's 'Deep Space' Programme.[143]

After Christoforo privately confirmed the authenticity of the Jesuit, a meeting was arranged. At this meeting, the Jesuit revealed more about the Deep Space Programme, which was classified as 'Secretum Omega' - the highest classification of secrecy inside the Vatican. The Deep Space Programme involved launching an infrared satellite named SILOE into space. The probe eventually approached the large planet then returned to Earth. On its way back in 1995, SILOE started to relay its images via a powerful radio telescope based in Alaska.[144] The SIV, working in partnership with Lockheed Martin, had launched the probe from Area 51 using an electro-magnetic impulse motor.

The Jesuits later analysed the Alaskan data that revealed an enormous celestial body, whose presence, he said, would be felt around 2004.* The Jesuit then shared information about the growing conflict going on behind Vatican walls between those who wish to disclose this information, and others with fixed interests, who wish to keep it secret. He said 'We are crazy, splintered according to the system, but we know that certain events are going to happen to all living beings on the planet; no-one is excluded.[145] All humanity in this actual period of history is living in a particular circumstance and intimately linked to some key events contained in the book of the Apocalypse. The human race must surrender completely to the message of salvation and redemption of Christ.' *According to the US Geological Survey (USGS) 2004, was the deadliest year for earthquakes since the Renaissance Age. The total loss of life from earthquakes was 276,856, with a 9.0 earthquake and subsequent Tsunami that took place in the Indian Ocean on December 26th.

In his book 'Petrus Romanus the Final Pope is Here,' Tom Horn and Cris Putnam studied the prophecies of Bishop Malachi of Armagh. In 1104, Malachi was summoned to Rome by Pope Celestine 2nd. On his journey he became deeply moved by the abject poverty he saw around him. In contrast, the Papacy and Cardinals were surrounded with all the trappings of wealth, and this sickened him. As he was leaving the city, he fell into a trance and his utterances were recorded by another attending cleric. In these prophecies Malachi was given a clue to a particular characteristic of each Pope or Papacy.

The last Pope would be the 112th and become known as 'Peter the Roman.' 'In the extreme persecution of the Holy Roman Church, there will sit Peter the Roman, who will pasture his sheep during many tribulations. And when these things are finished, the city of 'seven hills' will be destroyed, and the terrible judge will judge his people.' Studying documentation on

Malachi's prophecies led Horn to go 'on the record' that the penultimate Pope Benedict would resign his position, something that hadn't happened for five hundred years. Benedict resigned a year *after* the book Petrus Romanus was published.

Although Pope Francis, our current and potentially last Pope is unwell, and does not easily fit into the role of 'Peter the Roman', one of Francis's first visits after succession, was to the Clementine Chapel where he was deeply moved, and according to Cardinal Comastri, that as the Pope walked out from the chapel, 'At that moment, we had the distinct impression that the life of Peter rose out of centuries past and became present and living in the current successor of the Apostle Peter.'

The Book of Revelation chapter 17 provides insight into the final days of the Popish Church. In verses 4 and 5 we see a prostitute sitting on a scarlet beast that was full of blasphemous names and had seven heads and ten horns. The woman is clothed with purple and scarlet (the colour of religious vestments) and adorned with gold and jewels and pearls, holding in her hand a golden cup full of abominations and the impurities of her fornication. In verse 9, Rome is identified as 'Mystery Babylon,' as she is seated where the seven hills of Rome are located.

The worship of the mother and child goes back to antiquity and is derived from the worship of Nimrod who was supposedly reborn as the child Tammuz after Nimrod's wife, the prostitute Semiramis, was found to be with child after his death.[146] She claimed that Nimrod had appeared to her in spirit form and had been re-incarnated as the Sun God. Semiramis and Tammuz have been venerated in different guises ever since. Followers of Tammuz made the sign of a letter 'T' on their chests as a physical representation of their allegiance. It's not a coincidence that in Catholic ceremonies and processions, the sun shaped communion wafer is carried in something called a monstrance,[147] a receptacle that looks like a sunburst, nor that monks sometimes have the centre of their heads shaved to represent the shape of the sun. The pine cone on display at the Vatican and on the Pope's staff is an ancient symbol represented in many esoteric religions, especially those of Egypt and Babylon, as the opening of the third eye of spiritual (occult) understanding.[148]

The pineal gland in the brain, which is shaped like a tiny unopened pine cone, was thought to be the bridge between the physical and spiritual world, which would open when certain spiritual exercises were conducted. Just as a prostitute accepts the favours of many men, so 'Mystery Babylon' will receive into its communion, regardless of their belief systems, all other religious faiths, 'New Age' cults and organisations, that have been left behind after the rapture of the church.

Chapter 20

Obedience Tools of the New World Order 1 – Weather Warfare

Operation Indigo Skyfold: Although chemical spraying is nothing new, and was tested back in the 1920's with biplanes being used to spray smoke screens to gain a tactical advantage on the battlefield, it has never before been used on this scale as a biological warfare weapon against humanity, and reveals the government's tacit acceptance of the need to 'cull the herd.' Hypocritical government leaders are all complicit in this act, and while they publically wring their hands begging us to reduce our CO_2 emissions, thousands of tons of poisonous particulates are being sprayed over our heads every day, in a desperate effort not only to reduce the world's population, but to also reduce the effects of the earth's tilt, which is now shifting precariously in it's relation to the Sun.[149]

In 1993 the first few commercial jets were re-fitted with additional nozzles, and spraying tests took place in the United States. Huge tanks of chemicals were loaded onto military tanker aircraft that had been retro fitted with external nozzles. These chemicals were a toxic mix of aluminium, strontium and barium salts. Early tests also included polymers, animal blood and metallic filaments. As more aeroplanes commenced their spraying activities, the effects on those being sprayed became intolerable.[150]

It was in the late 1990's and early 2000's when the first effects of chemical spraying really begun to take its toll.[151] On

December 31ˢᵗ 2000, The Idaho Observer highlighted the work of chemtrail researcher Clifford Carnicom who found high levels of metallic alkaline salts in rainfall samples collected across the United States. Ph levels data tests showed that ion concentration had increased to over twenty times its previous levels within a single year since chemtrail spraying had started, and that the identification of barium in the atmosphere was as a result of aircraft aerosol spraying activities.

On January 21ˢᵗ 1999, The Lancet reported that meningitis cases in Britain reached a fifty year high with four hundred and forty notifications in the first three weeks in January, compared with two hundred and twenty for the same period in 1998. While on January 8ᵗʰ 2000, The Daily Telegraph reported that 'Refrigerated Lorries are once again being used by the NHS as temporary morgues in a grim repetition of scenes outside hospitals last winter. Hospitals on Britain's south coast were forced to store bodies in trailers after nearly 40% of elderly victims of *pneumonia contracted from an* 'inflenza-like' illness, *died*' (italics mine).[152] On the ground, people started filling up hospitals suffering from a mysterious 'flu like' disease. A resident of the Isle of Man found, returning to his small island community, after an absence of twenty-two years that the health of the islanders had dramatically changed. Some had died or developed a number of health conditions including very bad viruses, colds or pneumonia. This, he thought, was strange as the island does not have any polluting industries but is located under main airline routes.[153] He noted that a number of these illnesses started around 1993.

Another testimonial: one woman whose blood platelets were down by half wrote, I live in a rural community and most of these people have worked outside their whole lives and have never experienced these kind of symptoms. That is until the contrails started showing up last fall. We live in a no flight area,

114

yet it is not uncommon to see up to fifty contrails a day flying the multiple line patterns and the 'X' pattern. Referring to her illness, she added, 'Not just the usual sicknesses. Doctors have no idea what's causing them and have no cure for them. We had two children die here from totally unrelated illnesses when the contrails were flying all the time. We have dead birds in our yards, we have dead animals. The livestock is sick. Suddenly, last winter, my nine year old daughter came down with an asthma problem out of the blue.'[154]

During this time a number of victims of 'chemtrail flu' testified of seeing thousands of web-like filaments falling from the sky and attaching to plants, houses and telephone poles. Once handled, they quickly disintegrated but often caused the handler to become unwell. People who had the samples tested found that the filaments contained polymers and acetates but then it seemed to quickly disintegrate and could not be confirmed.[155]

All of a sudden, hospitals started to fill up with people suffering from a serious respiratory 'flu-like' disease, and a raft of illnesses like ME (disparagingly called yuppie flu), asthmatic conditions and Morgellan's 'disease' where filaments from chemtrail aeroplanes entered the victim's bloodstream and became active around microwaves.[156] How many 'allergies' suddenly appeared around that time, as people's immune systems became shot to pieces? Some people just felt 'under the weather' for weeks or months at a time.

A cloud seeding patent for modifying clouds was applied for shortly after these incidents took place.

United States Patent No US 6,315,213 B1 Dated November 13th 2001

Abstract: A method for artificially modifying the weather by seeding rain clouds of a storm with suitable cross-linked aqueous polymer. The polymer is dispersed in the cloud and the wind of the storm agitates the mixture causing the polymer to absorb the rain. The reaction forms a glutinous substance which precipitates to the surface below; thus diminishing the clouds' ability to rain.

Obedience Tools of The New World Order 2 – Space, Psychotronic and Financial Control Systems

1984, the year that George Orwell identified as a world dictatorship run by 'Big Brother', and just a year after NASA secretly concluded that Nibiru's orbit would decimate our planet, a readiness exercise called Rex 84 took place.[157] The Globalists had developed a two point plan. 1) To work with world governments and help them to prepare for the approaching set of major disasters and 2) Develop a believable environmental narrative and grand deception to control the masses that would start to wonder why the earth was in a state of collapse.[157] The Rex 84 exercise involved FEMA working in association with thirty-four federal civil departments and alongside other NATO nations that conducted a series of preparation exercises between April 5th and April 13th. These drills anticipated civil disturbances, major disruptions, strikes and demonstrations that would undermine the government's ability to rule effectively, and how this would disrupt resource management. To fight expected subversive individuals, those who were identified as 'trouble makers' would be rounded up. The government would also suspend the American constitution and implement Martial Law with civilians being removed from their homes and taken to designated holding areas.

In case the White House is destroyed by incoming asteroids and to ensure continuity of government, a new base has been built in a safer area. In 1995 Denver Airport was finally constructed. At 35,000 acres, it is twice the size as its nearest rival and was sixteen months behind schedule and over $2 billion over budget.[158] The dedication of the airport took place on March 19th 1994 and the dedication stone shows the Masonic symbol of a compass with the letter G inside, which has a link to the IG Farben Company who were directly involved with the Nazi's and the Holocaust.[158] The 'New World Airport Commission' is recognised as having helped to fund and build the airport. A statue of a blue deranged looking horse has been placed just outside the airport that has been nicknamed 'Blucifer.' The horse's sculptor, Luis Jimenez, died when part of the large fibreglass model fell on him at his studio in Hondo, New Mexico, severing an artery.[159] There are also a number of bizarre murals created by Leo Tangumas inside the airport alluding to some sort of future apocalyptic event. A gas masked alien Nazi is seen stabbing a dove of peace with a Muslim sabre in front of a new age rainbow chemtrail, with people below suffering from toxicity and genocide (see picture gallery). Against the backdrop of a near extinction event, children are seen weeping over three open caskets. The funeral service is for the black African people on the left, the native Indians in the middle and the white Judeo Christians on the right. The airport also features an animatronics talking gargoyle who welcomes visitors with 'Hi' and 'Welcome to Illumanati Headquarters... cough... err... I mean Denver International Airport!'[160]

What series of catastrophic future world events are the Elite planning for, that would cause them to construct such a strange airport unless it will become a de-facto headquarters during when world conditions become intollerable. It is also surprising that, given its location, it had over twenty-eight million visitors in 2021, making it the third most visited airport in the United States.[161] Speculation for the delay, and spiralling costs, were thought to be due to the underground bunkers they wanted to include. Those who planned it know that we are very close to the time period that the Bible calls 'The Great Tribulation.'

In September 2000, a report entitled 'Project for a New American Century Rebuilding America's Defences' was released, which stated that to 'further the process of transformation, even if it brings revolutionary change, is likely to be a long one, *absent some catastrophic and catalysing event- like a new Pearl Harbour'* (italics mine). Of course, a year later, an event like a new 'Pearl Harbour' did occur when a 'false flag' attack on the Twin Towers took place, which led to the US and UK 's 'War Against Terror' in Afghanistan, and it's tragic debacle.

The plan was to weaken American democracy and develop worldwide panic. 9/11 wounded America's psyche and gave the Elite the results they had hoped for. It showed that the world's strongest democracy was unable to protect its own citizens from a terrorist threat. Changes took place that brought us to the next stage of totalitarian control as the world went into travel lockdown. People came to accept that certain civil liberties needed to be surrendered for peace and safety. In the UK, armed guards became a regular feature in most of our airports.

It could be argued that 9/11 gave legitimacy to change parts of the American Constitution that the Elite found a hindrance to imposing totalitarian control and wished to supersede it. This includes the 'Patriot Act.'[162] This spying charter found agreement in The House of Representatives and could, under certain circumstances, allow the US Government to spy on anyone and record their telephone conversations. They could now read any form of communication without recourse to law. This would also allow the indefinite detention without trial of any immigrant it considered a threat. This act has been amended a number of times and in 2015 the scope of the bill was increased.[163]

Not only was there a 'mission creep' of laws eroding our democracy, on the ground, a new form of space warfare was being deployed by the Military Industrial Complex to control and coerce certain individuals using satellites and psychotronic weaponry. In 2001, efforts were made by a number of concerned Senators, including Dennis Kucinich, to pass a law, which would provide a basic level of protection for the American public and prevent the hijacking of space. However, like so many other laws that try to protect the public and curb the flagrant disregard the M.I.C. have for rules and regulations, this one was unable to find enough support from the Senators to pass the bill, but it provides insight into what is really going on in space.[164]

Space Preservation Act of 2001, 107 Congress 1st Session HR 2977

To preserve the cooperative, peaceful uses of space for the benefit of all humankind by permanently prohibiting the basing of weapons in space by the United States, and to require the President to take action to adopt and implement a world treaty banning space-based weapons.

In the House of Representatives October 2nd 2001

Sec. 3. Permanent Ban on Basing of Weapons in Space.

The President shall –

Implement a permanent ban on space-based weapons of the United States and remove from space any existing space-based weapons of the United States; and immediately order the permanent termination of research and development, testing, manufacturing, production, and deployment of all space-based weapons of the United States and their components.

120

Sec.7. Definitions.

(I) Inflicting death or injury on, or damaging or destroying, a person (or the biological life, bodily health, mental health, or physical and economic well-being of a person)

(II) Through the use of land-based, sea-based or space-based systems using radiation, electromagnetic, psychotronic, sonic, laser, or other energies *directed at individual persons or targeted populations for the purpose of information war, mood management, or mind control of such persons or populations; or* (italics mine)

(III) By expelling chemical or biological agents in the vicinity of a person;

(B) Such terms include exotic weapons systems such as –

   (i)   electronic, psychotronic, or information weapons;
   (ii)   chemtrails;
   (iii) high altitude ultra low frequency weapons systems;
   (iv)   plasma, electromagnetic, sonic, or ultrasonic weapons;
   (v)   laser weapons systems;
   (vi)   strategic, theatre, tactical, or extra-terrestrial weapons; and
   (vii) chemical, biological, environmental, climate, or tectonic weapons.

(C) The term 'exotic weapons systems' includes weapons designed to damage space or natural ecosystems (such as the ionosphere and upper atmosphere) or climate, weather, and tectonic systems with the purpose of inducing damage or destruction upon a target population or region on Earth or in space.

Just such a weapon would be the HAARP facility in Alaska, which has been involved in weather modification programmes for decades. The High frequency Active Auroral Research

Programme is a series of high frequency broadcast antennas, which agitates then heats up the ionosphere and has been instrumental in causing weather warfare, cloud modification, and the re-steering of our jet stream.

US Patent 4,686,605 Assignee BAE Systems

Method and apparatus for altering a region in the Earth's atmosphere, Ionosphere and or/magnetosphere.

Abstract: (part) A method and apparatus for altering at least one selected region, which normally exists above the Earth's surface. The region is excited by electron cyclonic resonance heating to thereby increase its charged particle density... the radiation is transmitted at a frequency with excited electronic cyclotronic resonance to heat and accelerate its charged particles.

Of course this device won't be used for turning arid regions of the world into fertile wetlands, or putting out forest fires in California, or prevent its recent flooding, quite the opposite. It is used for making fertile regions arid and reducing precipitation to ensure that main food producing areas have poor harvests. The NWO will use food scarcity as another tool in their social control playlist.

Researcher Michael Unum posted this revealing information on the Internet: One of the most impressive uses for the HAARP device is as an indirect fire energy weapon. The HAARP can create a steerable beam, which can burn temporary holes in our protective Ionosphere layer. This can cause a predictable corridor for the Sun's Gamma radiation pulse to get through this protective layer.[165]

Just think of the uses of such a weapon if, for instance, you wanted to control the weather and create a worldwide famine.

You could buy up farmland dirt cheap from drought laden impoverished farmers in America, and plant your own specially modified aluminium resistant genetically modified crops. You could then sell the land back to the farmers you stole it from in the first place as long as they agree to purchase your genetically altered seeds.

The Elite have developed a huge array of macro-scale weapons that can be used to determine a country's ability to sustain its food production. On a micro scale, a number of psychotronic brain disruptor obedience/control tools are at their disposal. This includes 'voice to brain' devices like the invention of the Neurophone by Dr Patrick Flanagan, US patents 3,393,279 & 3647,970, which converts sound into electrical impulses delivered via satellite against targeted individuals. Others include:

US Patent 6488617B1 Abstract: (part) Method and device for producing a design brain state in an individual that contains the means for monitoring and analysing the brain's state, while a set of one or more magnets produce fields that alter this state.

US patent 4616261A Abstract: (part) Method and apparatus for generating subliminal visual messages. A system for generating a subliminal message during the display of a normal television programme on a television receiver utilizes a personal computer to generate a RF carrier modulated with video signals encoding the subliminal message.

US patent 6506148 B2 Abstract: (part) Nervous system manipulation by electromagnetic fields from monitors. The image displayed on a computer monitor may be pulsed effectively by a simple computer programme. For certain monitors, pulsed electromagnetic fields capable of exciting sensory resonances in nearby subjects may be generated even as the displayed images are pulsed with subliminal intensity. Just imagine this programme running when an advert for gambling is shown.

These can be found on the Directed Energy Weapons (DEW)/ targeted individual patents website.

FINANCIAL CONTROL

The financial model that the Globalist conspirators are about to roll out worldwide, is an adaptation of the one currently being used by the Chinese Communist Government. Any perceived anti-government views expressed by individuals or the populace, will result in the reduction or suspension of financial payments and the inability to travel abroad. This will stay in place until 'social credits' can be built up again by individuals taking part in approved good community actions or other pro-government programmes.

On March 9th 2022, Joe Biden signed Executive Order 14067 into law.[166] Section 4 ordered *urgent* research into the development of the 'digital dollar', which is the first stage for *all* Western democracies, to develop Central Bank Digital Currency systems themselves. This new global financial control system will phase out all fiat (paper) transactions. It is currently unknown if both systems will run side by side for a few years, or if the Globalists are preparing another financial shock that will cause rampant inflation, which will in turn destroy the cash economy. This system will eventually come under the control of the Antichrist and will take the world through to the return of Jesus Christ on earth. The new system is being called the 'digital dollar' or 'Biden's Bucks' in the United States.

Once in place, with cash transactions becoming just a distant memory, they will be able to control with whom or on what you spend your finance. This world government run system can force you to:

Get vaccinated against your will, buy an electric car you don't want, purchase solar panels you don't need, ration your heat and water use by capping your usage every month, via your smart meter (to save the planet of course!), determine where or to whom you send your payments and what political party you financially support. They will even be able to prevent you going on strike or protesting against government oppression. As each digital currency will be a programmable token, any infraction against the state can lead to it being switched off. To disobey will lead to starvation.[167]

The FTX scandal and collapse resulting in $32 billion of crypto currencies being 'disappeared' or re-funnelled will be an excuse for all crypto currencies coming under tighter government controls.[168]

Chapter 22

Between a Rock and a Hard Place

Mankind has a date with destiny and that date is Friday 13th April 2029, when, according to NASA's calculations, a large asteroid called Apophis will either skim past the earth and destroy a number of orbiting satellites, or crash into earth causing a near extinction event. Apophis is travelling at 28,000 miles per hour, measures 317 metres across and is estimated to weigh a massive 20 million metric tons.[169] However, to avoid causing stress and alarm, NASA has been accused of intentionally skewing the figures to present us with a close flyby. So are we all safe or not? According to mathematician Harry Lear, NASA made a serious miscalculation on this future event, and he sent a letter to previous incumbent President Trump asking them to reformulate their findings. Apophis is appropriately named after the Egyptian god of chaos and destruction.[170]

The earth has started to go through a significant asteroid field and the number of 'near misses' is increasing. Some of these Near Earth Objects are potential planet killers. Up to 70% of space rocks get through undetected and are travelling so fast that, even if they were found in time, nothing could be done to change their trajectory. At Chelyabinsk in 2013, a meteor exploded in the sky over Russia causing serious damage and injury, when the whole area was rocked and windows blew out, injuring 1,500 people.

The NEOWISE Wide Field Infrared Survey Explorer Space Telescope was launched in 2009. Its mission, just like the IRAS satellite in 1983, was to survey the sky in infrared to detect NEO's that could present a threat to Earth. It collected data on the size, shape, distance and potential threat. These objects are then classified by Spaceguard.[171] Formed in 1998, Spaceguard is a collaboration between the UK, US and other nations to gather the information required to take action. If a space rock was over 460 feet long across, it was classified as a Potentially Hazardous Object. In 1990, only 134 Near Earth Asteroids were detected by scientists, with forty-two being classified as a PHO. By 1st January 2022, they had observed 27,820 asteroids with 2,230 being considered a PHO.[172] Asteroids, no larger than sixty-six feet diameter can cause serious damage to our environment and have a devastating effect on local infrastructure, so just imagine what a one kilometre rock would do. 90% of the asteroids that have so far been detected are over a kilometre long. With the help of NEOWISE, NASA were able to predict that a small Asteroid 2022 EB5 would hit the Norwegian Sea, but without causing any significant damage.

Although NASA continues to claim that Apophis will not hit the earth in 2029, a draft report issued on November 9th 2022, by the Apophis Specific Action Team, tells a different story. The group was formed at the request of NASA's Planetary Science Division. Its executive summary states; that 'while the Apophis earth close approach has been modelled by several authors, the quantative details of the predictive effects vary from model to model and are, in general, sensitive to uncertainties about Apophis's shape, internal structure, and rotation state during the close approach. As a result it is not currently possible to definitively quantify the likely outcome of the close approach. The report also revealed that as it approaches the earth; '*The asteroids orbit will definitely change and its spin state will most likely undergo a significant change.*' (Italics mine).

By contrast, The planet Nibiru *will not* hit the earth but its enormous gravitational influence is already causing the earth to wobble on its axis. Environmental chaos will continue as this object transits our Sun and then gathers pace to shoot its way back into deep space. However, Apophis or some other NEO named Wormwood in scripture *will* hit the Earth. It will cause extreme destruction that develops into something that closely resembles a nuclear winter, causing failed harvests. If Apophis is not currently heading for a direct hit on earth, it would only take a small knock from another space rock to alter its trajectory, so it is not possible to determine what will happen, regardless what NASA claims.

Some biblical scholars are linking the asteroid Apophis with Wormwood, which is mentioned in the Book of Revelation 8:7–11. 'The first angel sounded his trumpet, and there came hail and fire mixed with blood, and it was hurled down upon the earth. A third of the earth was burned up, a third of the trees were burned up, and all the green grass was burned up. The second angel sounded his trumpet and something like a huge mountain, all ablaze, was thrown into the sea. A third of the sea turned to blood; a third of the living creatures in the sea died and a third of the ships were destroyed. The third angel sounded his trumpet, and a great star, blazing like a torch fell from the sky on a third of the rivers and the springs of waters and the name of the star is Wormwood. A third of the waters turned bitter, and many people died from the waters that had become bitter.'

'Immediately after the suffering of those days, the Sun will be darkened and the Moon will not give its light. The stars (asteroids) will fall from Heaven, and the powers of Heaven will be shaken.' Matthew 24:29

Mathew 24:7: 'But about that day or hour no one knows, neither the angels of Heaven, nor the Son, but only the Father. For as the days of Noah were, so will be the coming of the Son of Man. For in those days before the flood, they were eating and drinking, marrying and giving in marriage, until the day Noah entered the ark, and they knew nothing until the flood came and swept them all away. So too will be the coming of the Son of Man.'

It is still possible that Apophis will be a close 'flyby' and everyone breathes a huge sigh of relief. What you *must know* is this: If the church of Jesus Christ is still on the earth throughout 2029, then because of God's people, the earth will be spared. If, however, the rapture *has occurred* before 2029 and over a billion people just suddenly 'disappear,' then the earth hasn't been spared and God's judgements, that include a massive asteroid called Wormwood hitting the earth, are about to commence.

Chapter 23

Biblical Patterns and Parallels

'What has happened before will happen again. What has been done before will be done again. There is nothing new in the whole world.' Ecclesiastes 1:9 Good News Bible

So what parallels can we observe in the ancient world to ours that give us clues and guide posts to help us navigate future events? Enoch lived for 365 years on the earth - one year for each day in our Gregorian calendar. Like Elijah, he was taken physically up to Heaven and is a type of the rapture of the church, and will return to earth as one of the two witnesses mentioned in Revelation Chapter 11: 3–8. Back on earth, they witness to the nations for one thousand two hundred and sixty days, or 3.5 years. Ancient calendars define a year as 360 days. They also prophesy and have power to bring judgements upon the earth. After this, the Antichrist kills them, but their bodies remain unburied for 3.5 days. The breath of God raises them up, which shocks all the onlookers when they both ascend up to Heaven in a cloud, just as Christ did in Acts 1:9. This presents another sign to the Jews about Jesus being the true Messiah, after which a huge earthquake occurs just as it did after Christ's crucifixion.

Some of Enoch's writings were discovered in 1947 and were added to the partial book of Enoch found by explorer James Bruce when he visited a church in Ethiopia.[173] He found part of these ancient texts preserved as part of the church's scripture. The rest were found in cave four at Quarum when an Arab shepherd boy was searching for a lost goat. He threw stones into a cave and heard a pot smash and went in to investigate.[174] What is most significant about the timing of this discovery, is that the published book of Enoch translated by RH Charles has been specifically written for the encouragement of the 'Tribulation Saints,' which should signify to us that the tribulation, a time period of seven years, is about to begin and that Enoch's, Elijah's and Jesus Christ's return to earth is imminent!

Enoch 1:1-9 'The words of the blessing of Enoch, wherewith he blessed the elect and righteous *who will be living in the day of tribulation when all the wicked and godless are to be removed* (Not taken up like the church but destroyed on earth). And he took up his parable and said "Enoch a righteous man, whose eyes were opened by God, saw the vision of the Holy One in the heavens, which the angels showed me and from them I heard everything, and from them I understood as I saw, *but not for this generation, but for a remote one which is for to come.'* (Italics mine) Concerning the elect I said, and took up my parable concerning them:

'The Holy Great One will come forth from His dwelling, and the eternal God will tread upon the earth, even on Mount Sinai, and appear from His camp and appear in the strength of His might from the heaven of heavens, and all shall be smitten with fear, and the Watchers shall quake, and great fear and trembling shall seize them unto the ends of the earth. And the high mountains shall be shaken, and the high hills shall be made low and shall melt like wax before a flame. And the earth shall be wholly rent in sunder, and all that is on the earth shall perish, and there shall be judgement upon all men. But with the righteous He shall make peace, and will protect the elect, and mercy shall be upon them. And they shall all belong to God, and they shall be prospered, and they shall all be blessed. And He shall help them all, and light shall appear unto them, and He will make peace with them.'

'And behold! He cometh with ten thousands of His holy ones to execute judgement upon all, and to destroy all the ungodly, and to convict all flesh of all the works of ungodliness, which they the ungodly have committed, and of all the hard things, which ungodly sinners have spoken against Him.' This last sentence is quoted in the book of Jude.

Numbers have a huge significance in Bible prophecy and when studying the scriptures and looking back historically, we can see a number of patterns being weaved by God. According to Jasher 7:51, Abraham was born 1,948 years from Adam, while the nation Israel was 'born' (came into existence) in 1948 AD. This fulfilled Isaiah 66:8 'Who has ever heard of such things? Who has ever seen things like this? Can a country be born in a day or a nation be brought forth in a moment? Yet no sooner is Zion in labour than she gives birth to her children.'

Abraham fled and hid from Nimrod. Jasher 12:60: Just as the Jews will flee from the 'resurrected' Antichrist after the murder of Elijah and Enoch, and go into hiding as mentioned in Matthew 24 15-22 AV, 'When ye shall therefore see the abomination of desolation, spoken by Daniel the prophet, stand in the holy place, (whoso readeth, let him understand) then let them that be in Judea flee into the mountains. Let him which is on the house top not come down to take anything out of his house. Neither let him which is in the field return back to take his clothes. And woe to them that are with child, and to them that give suck in those days! But pray that your flight be not in the winter, neither on the Sabbath day. For then shall be great tribulation, such as was not since the beginning of the world to this time, no, nor ever shall be. And except these days shall be shortened, there should no flesh be saved, but for the elect's sake, those days shall be shortened.'

One of the most significant biblical numbers is 4 and multiples of it is often related to a time of testing and judgement. In the book of Revelation we read about the four horsemen of the Apocalypse. Moses killed an Egyptian at the age of 40, spent 40 years in the wilderness looking after sheep, and then 40 years looking after more 'bleating 'sheep,' as he took the nation of Israel around the wilderness. There is a gap of 400 years between the last prophet Malachi and the birth of Christ. Incidentally, the last word in the Old Testament is 'curse.' While Christ our redeemer saves believers from the curse and judgement, and he was 40 days and nights being tempted by the devil in the wilderness.

Jesus told us that the last days on earth would resemble the days of Noah. In Genesis we learn that Noah was a preacher of righteousness and that he preached for 120 years, (3 x 40), but no one listened and only his family were saved. He also told us of a time period called the 'beginning of sorrows' as a time of great tragedy and loss but that the end would not be yet. Matthew 24:8

After the disciples saw Jesus returning to Heaven, there were 120 people gathered in the upper room in prayer and awaiting for the empowerment of the Holy Spirit, Acts 1:15. God also reduced man's longevity to 120 years in Genesis 6 due to man's sin, later reducing it again to 70 years plus.

1917– The signing of the Balfour Declaration on November 2nd. A letter was sent by Arthur Balfour to Lord Rothschild, which proposed providing a homeland for the Jews. Could this be the starting of the 'Beginning of Sorrows' period as mentioned by Jesus? World War 1 was still in progress. Three multiples of 40 will take us to the year 2037.

1906 - The great Azuza Street revival started in 1906 – add 120 years, this takes us to the year 2026. This last day's revival could come through the global introduction of the new cashless financial system, leading Christian believers to finally realise that this new system will shortly be aligned to the Antichrist. It could also be the realisation that dramatic earth changes are a precursor to God's judgements on mankind. This will create a deeper, closer reliance on God to meet our needs, and a fresh outpouring of God's Holy Spirit on the church is expected as it waits in anticipation to meet the Lord in the air. 1 Thessalonians 4:17

1948 - The birth of the State of Israel. Add 2 x 40 years to this date and you get to the year 2028, Israel's 80th anniversary year. A significant scripture which describes the length of one generation is mentioned in Psalm 90:10-12 and is introduced as 'The prayer of Moses.' *The days of our life are seventy years or perhaps eighty,* if we are strong; even then their span is only toil and trouble; *they are soon gone and we fly away.* Who considers the power of your anger? Your wrath is as great as the fear that is due to you. *So teach us to count our days that we may gain a wise heart.'* Will 2028 end one phase in Israel's history and start another?

In 2018 the United States moved their embassy to Jerusalem and Jared Kushner started the process of signing a number of peace treaties between the Jews and Arab nations. What is interesting is that another Jared is mentioned in Genesis 5:18 and in Hebrew the name 'yarad' means to fall or cast down. Like Elijah, Jared's son, Enoch was translated into Heaven without dying. Will this Jared be on the world stage again in 2028 to confirm his peace treaty? Jared is currently working with Arab countries, signing them up to the Abraham Accord, an agreement which provides a way forward for both Jews and Arabs to work together in harmony. Could 2028 be the same year that the church of Jesus Christ 'flies away'?

Chapter 24

Down the Rabbit Hole
(With Apologies to Lewis Carroll)

You will be forgiven for thinking that over the last decade we have all collectively fallen down a very dark and deep rabbit hole and landed in a place where nothing makes sense anymore. As we dust ourselves off, we meet the white rabbit who is running out of time and is very late for an appointment, so we scurry behind. As we rush towards our unknown destination, we suddenly feel that we are being watched, not realising that our every move is being monitored by the invisible 'Cheshire Cat' surveillance system. As we approach a large table, we meet 'The Mad Hatter' and his cronies, who are trying to implement 'Agenda 2030' protocols, and confuse everyone by celebrating everybody's un-birthday.

He says that he rules this alternative kingdom and you are to think in a very different way that you have ever thought before. He announces that you must:

Believe that a person's sex is not fixed at birth and that anyone can choose to be a boy, girl, male or female from the age of four. If any boy puts on a dress and changes his name from Gerald to Geraldine, every teacher must acknowledge this change and allow 'her' to use the girls' toilet; Anyone who believes that a child is best brought up in a caring loving family with married parents rather than a 'blended family' should be vilified, bullied and intimidated;

Any Professor who contends that there was anything positive about our colonial past should be constantly harassed and his life made a misery, and any colonial landmarks should be relocated into the river.

The late Queen's picture should be removed from our universities if it makes anyone feel 'uncomfortable.'

Anyone that doesn't 'take the knee' is a closet racist.

People should be allowed to marry whoever or whatever they want as long as it makes them happy.

Just using cash will cause you to be treated with suspicion.

Anyone who tries to put forward any other alternatives than the Mad Hatter's rules will be de-platformed and debunked by paid 'fact checker' stooges and have their Facebook, Twitter feeds and YouTube accounts frozen.

Meat eaters should be re-educated and provided with tasteless vegetarian alternatives.

Farmers should not plant crops anymore but let their farms go to 'rack and ruin' under 're-wilding' initiatives.

Only green compliant electric vehicles will be allowed to use certain roadways, the rest of us will end up using cramped highly taxed secondary alternatives.

No doubt in the future, anyone who has the privilege of owning a garden will have to share it with others under some Mad Hatter 'shared green space' initiative, leaving you to pick up their used cans of special brew and cigarette ends out of your petunias once they leave! To 'save the planet' we must all reduce our greenhouse emissions and eventually move away from our country dwellings to Artificial Intelligence controlled mega sized 'Smart Cities,' where every move is monitored. Anyone not complying with the Mad Hatter's rules will be sent to the White Queen of broken hearts and have their heads lopped off!

The books by Aldous Huxley, Brave New World, George Orwell's 1984 and the television series 'The Prisoner,' all present us with nightmare visions of our future. In the book '1984' a man named Winston Smith battles against the totalitarian state of Oceania where 'Big Brother' controls all activities. The apparatus of the state includes 'The Ministries Of Truth' that advocates lies and propaganda; 'Love,' a Ministry involved with torture and oppression; 'Plenty' that keeps the population in a condition of near starvation, and 'Peace' that keeps the military in a state of perpetual war.

Winston falls in love with Julia and speaks to a man called O'Brien about his affair. They believe that O'Brien is part of a subversive brotherhood, and are given a book by Emmanuel Goldstein who used to be a friend of Big Brother but then turned against him. However, they realise too late that O'Brien is a government agent and Winston is taken to Room 101 where he is tortured using his fear of rats. Winston's will is finally broken and he learns to love 'Big Brother' and becomes subservient to the state.[175]

In Brave New World, Huxley anticipates huge changes in reproductive health. Infants are born from womb like test tubes at birthing centres that resemble hatcheries. Embryos are tested and then chemically enhanced to determine their future caste based on tests to determine their levels of intelligence. Some go on to become Alpha Plus, future leaders, while others are chemically changed to become Delta's or Epsilons, a caste of lower valued 'worker drones.' Sexual permissiveness is encouraged as is Soma, the drug of choice to alleviate social boredom. The world controller is Mustapa Mond who, rather than torturing people who resist his world view, exiles them instead to islands like the Falklands, which he considers is 'full of the most interesting people in the world' and is the fate of all those who do not fit into his model of the world state.[176]

In the Prisoner, a television series from the 1960's, a Secret Service agent resigns, returns home and is gassed into unconsciousness. He then wakes up in what he thinks is his flat. He walks groggily to the window, then realises that everything has changed. He has been transported to 'The Village,' a cashless society, where people are issued with weekly work units. Information is controlled and he can only purchase a *local* paper or map. He can't get hold of a self-drive car and can only ride in taxis. It is a surveillance society where everyone has a designated number. His is number 6 and everything he does is monitored from the moment he wakes up to the time he goes to bed.

The Village is a place where free speech is eroded. When Number 6 challenges the mindset of the village's poetry society, he is considered mentally unstable and is referred to the social welfare group. He is eventually classified as a threat to The Village, and his phone, water and electrics supply are all switched off. The villagers' patience finally runs out and they forcibly take him to the hospital where he is due to receive 'instant social conversion,' a laser incision into his frontal lobe. While Number 6 remains in 'The Village,' he spends his time trying to outwit Number 2 and discovering who 'Number 1' is, the unseen real power broker working behind the scenes.[177]

Chapter 25

The Last Two Churches

In the book of Revelation, the last two churches to be mentioned are one residing at Laodicea and the other at Philadelphia. The church at Laodicea was in a prosperous city that boasted of its riches and its need of nothing, which included Jesus, who is pictured knocking at the door of the church trying to gain entry. From Christ's perspective, the congregation was wretched, pitiable, poor, blind and naked. The message for those who were able to listen was to repent, purchase the white garments of purity and to live a life refined by the Holy Spirit, just as gold is refined to remove all impurities.

The Philadelphian church of brotherly love had discerned that some of their congregation were bringing in false doctrine and rejected them. Some of the threats to the early church were the Christian cults of the Nicolatians (that believed in sexual expression outside of marriage was permissible) and the Gnostics (who believed that the material world was evil, and that 'Gnosis' or spiritual insight or knowledge transcended church teaching and doctrine). They preferred the ideas of illusion and enlightenment to sin and repentance.

The Philadelphia church is offered an open door and is told that, 'because you have kept my word of patient endurance, I will keep you from the hour of trial that is coming on the whole world to test the inhabitants of the earth.' This prophecy had a partial fulfilment in the church's deliverance from Caesar's persecution; however, they are also a type of the raptured church. The hour of trial for all humanity will soon be upon us and we are offered the same open door as they were. This church is encouraged to hold firm to the faith so that God will write on them 'the name of my God and the name of the city of my God, the new Jerusalem that comes down from my God out of heaven and my new name.' Just as Satan will use the Antichrist to place his mark on the hands and heads of the unbeliever, Christ will place his new name on those who overcome Satan as we become citizens of the New Jerusalem.

In Revelation chapter 4, a door is opened in Heaven and we hear a trumpet sound as a voice calls out 'Come up here and I will show you what must take place after this.' (This verse means after true believers are removed from the earth.) From Chapter 4 onwards the word church does not appear and all that are left on the Earth are the following:

1) The rebellious, unrepentant sinners who are about to be marked by the Antichrist. This mark will somehow change their genetic code and install satanically manipulated DNA, making those left behind some sort of chimeras (not fully human and therefore unable to be redeemed).

2) The 144,000 Jewish evangelists, who will be sealed by God and preach the message of salvation and who will be martyred for refusing to take the devil's mark.

3) The two witnesses, Enoch and Elijah, who presumably return to earth at the same time as the 144,000 evangelists, and who prophecy for 1,260 days.

4) Repentant tribulation saints- Those who do not receive the Antichrist's mark but will not be able to buy or sell anything during the tribulation period, and will eventually be martyred by guillotine and be forever with the Lord. Those who receive the 'mark', becoming chimeras, will spend eternity in Hell.

Chapter 26

Satan's Busted Flush

Jeremiah 2:13 'For my people have committed two evils: they have forsaken me, the fountain of living water, and dug out cisterns for themselves, cracked cisterns that can hold no water.'

The Bible has a lot to say about dramatic changes in both our physical and spiritual world just before Christ returns, and these are a part of the pattern of God's judgements on sinful mankind. We are about to experience a number of existential threats that have been kept from us by demonic entities that use the occult controlled media to cover things up.

As man has rejected our wonderful Creator, in his permissive will, God will allow the evil, deluded and yet tragic fallen angel Satan, the 'god of the broken cisterns' who thought he could rise to Heaven and dislodge God from his Throne, a chance to provide fallen man with viable alternatives. These are:

A hybrid bible with more truth being erased by demonic experiments at CERN. However, the basic Bible message of Jesus dying on the cross and the need to repent is so far untarnished.

An alternative Creation Story: Through the Hadron Collider, Satan and his sinful band of arrogant, proud, scientific misfits have created in microcosm the 'Big Bang,' but this time turning order into chaos as the world and our sense of reality continues to unravel.

An alternative environment: Courtesy of the HAARP antennas based in Alaska, and thousands of aircraft pilots who have complied with NWO depopulation objectives, as they actively pour thousands of tons of harmful chemicals over our heads every day, and terra-form our once beautiful world.

An alternative food source: Due to the development of genetically modified foods, people can now eat food that has been artificially manipulated and is just about as far removed from the organic food that God intended man to eat. Monsanto have developed crops that are resistant to aluminium particulates.

An alternative Financial System: The coming cashless 'Mark of the Beast' Central Bank Digital Currency system will involve taking some sort of QR code or microchip that contains genetically manipulated DNA. This material will ultimately change mankind into unredeemable chimeras.

An alternative Religious System: The Babylonian/Catholic Cult is the largest in the world, as through its Mass it provides a wafer to its congregation in the shape of the sun; it secretly worships the sun god Tammuz. The Book of Revelation says that the Beast, The Antichrist, takes the false religious system, represented as the whore of Babylon for a short ride, initially working together. Halfway through his reign, he then destroys the false church, claiming that he is God incarnate. God's word for any latter day Catholics is this, 'Come out of her, my people, so that ye be not partakers of her sins, that ye be not partakers of her plagues.' Revelation 18:4 AV

An alternative 'Alien Rapture': As Satan can disguise himself as an 'Angel of Light,' then it is plausible that fallen angels can disguise themselves as our Nordic looking 'space brothers' who are visiting us from different worlds, and materialising from a different dark dimension, (just like the watchers did when they fell from grace and took human form in Genesis 6). They will claim that they are here to help humanity at our time of greatest need. These demonic counterfeits sometimes use biblical language, and are channelling their messages to their New Age gurus, preparing their followers for the rapture of the Christian church. In her book 'Bringers of the new dawn' Barbara Merciniac states;

'If human beings do not change – if they do not make the shift in values and realise that without earth they could not be here – then earth, in its love for its own initiation and its reaching for a higher frequency, will bring about a cleansing that will balance it once again. **There is the potential for many people to leave the planet in an afternoon.** Maybe then everyone else will begin to wake up to what is going on.'

She continues; 'As we see it, as the probable worlds begin to form, there will be great shiftings within humanity on this planet. It will seem that great chaos and turmoil are forming, that nations are rising against each other in war, and that earthquakes are happening more frequently. It will seem as if everything is falling apart and cannot be put back together. Just as you sometimes have rumblings and quaking in your lives as you change your old patterns and move into new energies, earth is shaking itself free, and a certain realignment or adjustment period is to be expected. It will also seem that the animals and fish are departing earth. Those animals are now moving over to the new world as it is being formed. They are not ending their existence; they are merely slipping into the new world to await your joining them.'

'Our rescue ships will be able to come in close enough in the twinkling of an eye to set the lifting beams in operation in a moment. And all over the globe where events warrant it, this will be the method of evacuation. Mankind will be lifted, levitated shall we say, by the beams from our smaller ships. These smaller craft will in turn taxi the persons to the larger ships overhead, higher in the atmosphere, where there is ample space and quarters and supplies for millions of people.' Quoted from Project World Evacuation 1993

An alternative Messiah: As the world continues to become unstable, and law and order breaks down, men will desperately seek a messianic figure, someone with answers who can resolve the Middle East conflict and bring peace to the world. Just as Antiochus Epiphanies used flattery, bringing a false sense of security to the Jews until he made his true intentions clear, so will the Antichrist, while the third Temple is being built. Halfway through his seven year reign, he stops the sacrifices and declares himself as God, demanding worship.

An alternative Resurrection: At some time during his reign, the Antichrist receives a mortal wound and is pronounced dead. The world is shocked into stunned silence. Here was the man that seemed to have all the political answers to the world's problems, and now he's dead. What will happen next?

An alternative Destiny: Rather than choosing to follow Christ, become born again and live in eternal bliss with their Creator, man has turned against God and decided to drink the stale water of sin from Satan's broken water cisterns. Unless he repents and returns to Christ, he will share the same fate as his unseen master and spend eternity in Hell with the devil and his angels.

The prophet Daniel was given a series of dreams about the formation of four future world empires. These have been identified as Babylon, Medo–Persia, Greece and Rome with a revised Rome re-emerging near the end. Many Bible scholars have identified the 'little horn' in Daniel chapter 8 as Antiochus Epiphanies who came from the Greek empire.

Possible future scenario: 'Today is a sad day for the world, as it has now been three days since the man who led the Middle East peace treaty and brought hope to the world, is 'Lying in State.' All world leaders are today paying their respects to our great leader as they slowly walk past the open glass sarcophagus in Jerusalem's chapel of rest.

Unknown to those attending, one of God's angels has been dispatched to the bottomless pit. He opens a door to the prison containing the bound spirit of Antiochus Epiphanies who returns to Jerusalem and enters the dead body of the Antichrist that is Lying in State.

One of the women in the crowd gasps! Was that a finger she saw twitching in the glass case or just a trick of the light? A few moments later, everyone looks on in amazement as the world leader, now possessed by the spirit of Epiphanies, rises from the dead and claims to be the resurrected saviour of the world. He then goes straight to the Jewish Temple and places his own image there (possibly a holographic projection or Avatar) and demands to be worshipped as God. He then turns his attention to the two prophets, Enoch and Elijah, who have been tormenting people with God's judgements and is allowed to kill them.

A brief recap on the Beast from the bottomless pit:

1) He had lived and died before John was born and will return to earth.
2) It is one of God's angels that releases the Beast from the bottomless pit, proving that God is still in control of world events.

3) The third Beast will be released halfway through the Tribulation Period.

4) Epiphanies returns to earth and declares himself as Divine and is represented as 'the little horn' in Daniel's vision.

5) He wages war against Elijah and Enoch and kills them in Jerusalem. After three days their unburied bodies are resurrected and they return to God.

6) History repeats itself as Antiochus pollutes God's sanctuary, this time by placing his own image in the rebuilt third temple.

7) He stops the red heifer sacrifices, claims to be God and forces the Jews to worship him.

8) He demands that everyone receives his mark, and anyone who does not is beheaded.

9) He institutes the destruction of the religious system throughout the world and murders the Babylonian/Catholic priests. See Revelation 17:12.

10) He now persecutes the Jews for three and a half years. They flee for their lives and possibly hide in Petra where they anxiously await the return of Jesus their true Messiah's return to earth.

Gamatria is a form of applying numbers to letters. The English form would be A=6, B=12 etc. Using this format, the words 'God Incarnate,' the name given to Epiphanies the King of Greece comes to 666. While in the Jewish language, the number is 340.

Looking up the Jewish form of Gamatria with references to the number 340, I noticed that a series of words that relate to end time events also total 340. These are: Nibiru ~ Human God ~Image of Satan ~ Chip Implant ~ Thumb ~ Third Coming ~Rome Pope ~ Life Decisions and Accepting Fate.

Chapter 27

Pre Rapture and Tribulation Prophecies

Many false 'Christ like' cult leaders and false prophets will arise that will lead people astray. This includes the Antichrist. Matthew 24:4-11

The World will become lawless and turn cold towards God. Matthew 24:12

People will turn against each other and betray them to the authorities. Matthew 24:9

Wars and ethnic conflicts will increase. Matthew 24:9

There shall be chaos also in many places, fire shall often break out, the wild animals shall roam beyond their haunts (animals will move into urban areas and attack people due to lack of food) and menstruating women will bring forth monsters (babies will be born deformed due to the increase in pollution and radiation on the earth). 2 Esdras 5-8

There will be huge disturbances in our seas and rivers. Luke 21:25

Pools of fresh water will be found in the sea. 2 Esdras 5-7 (This sign is in part happening now in the Dead Sea due to minerals being dug out.)

The tribulation period starts when the Antichrist signs a seven year peace deal between the Jews and Arabs. Jared Kushner's Abraham Accord? Daniel 9: 27

People will be seized with a great terror. 2 Esdras 5:1

The Sun and Moon will appear to shift from their orbits (pole shift). 2 Esdras 5:12

Further supporting evidence for the earth shifting on its axis just before Christ's return and its chaotic effects on our climate is found in Enoch 80: 2:6 'And in the days of the sinners, the years shall be shortened, and their seed shall be tardy on their lands and fields, *and all things on the earth shall alter, and not appear in their time.* And the rain shall be kept back, and the heaven shall withhold it. And in those times the fruits of the world will be backward, and not grow in their time, and the fruits of the trees shall be withheld in their time. And the Moon shall alter her order, and not appear at her time. And in those days the Sun shall be seen and he shall journey in the evening on the extremity of the great chariot in the west and shall shine more brightly than accords with the order of light. And many chiefs of the stars shall transgress the order prescribed. And these shall alter their orbits and tasks, and not appear at the seasons prescribed for them.' The sun, moon and stars appearing in different locations near the end will be how it appears to us, due to the earth's axis shift. The word 'tardy' means sluggish, delayed, consistently late, in arrears, derelict - the quality of being slow to understand the importance of their time on earth.

'The Sun and Moon shall eventually become darkened and asteroids will fall onto the earth.' Matthew 24:29 & 2 Esdras 5:5

'Blood rain will fall from the sky and our rivers and streams will turn blood red.' Revelation 16:6 & 2 Esdras 5:5

'The earth shall become a desolate trackless waste.' 2 Esdras 5:3

The unrepentant sinners left behind after the rapture of the church will grow furious with God and persecute new converts:

'The burning wrath of a great multitude is kindled over you. They shall drag some of you away and force some of you to eat what was sacrificed to idols. For in many places and neighbouring cities there shall be a great uprising against those who fear the Lord. They shall be like maniacs, sparing no one, but plundering and destroying those who continue to fear the Lord. For they shall destroy and plunder their goods and drive them out of house and home. Then the tested quality of my elect shall be manifest like gold that is tested by fire. Listen my elect ones, says the Lord. The days of tribulation are at hand but I will deliver you from them. Do not fear or doubt, for God is your guide. You who keep my commandments, and precepts, says the Lord, must not let your sins weigh you down, or your iniquities prevail over you.'2 Esdras 16:68 & 70-76

The horrifying future of this world is best described by Isaiah:

Isaiah 24:1-6 'Now the Lord is about to lay waste the earth and make it desolate. And he will twist its surface and scatter its inhabitants. And it shall be, as with the people, so with the priest, as with the slave, so with his master, as with the maid, so with her mistress, as with the buyer, so with the seller, as with the lender, so with the borrower, as with the creditor, so with the debtor. The earth shall be utterly laid waste and utterly despoiled, for the Lord has spoken in this word.'

'The earth dries up and withers, the world languishes and withers, the Heavens languish together with the earth. The earth lies polluted under its inhabitants, for they transgressed laws, violated the statutes, broken the everlasting covenant. Therefore, a curse devours the earth, and its inhabitants suffer for their guilt, therefore the inhabitants of the earth dwindled, and few people are left.'

Isaiah 24:17-23 'Terror, and the pit, and the snare are upon you, O inhabitant of the earth! Whoever flees at the sound of the terror shall fall into the pit, and whoever climbs out of the pit shall be caught in the snare. For the windows of Heaven are opened and the foundations of the earth tremble. The earth is utterly broken, the earth is torn asunder, and the earth is violently shaken. The earth staggers like a drunkard, it sways like a hut. Its transgression lies heavy upon it and it falls and will not rise again.'

God though, promises his people that they will be removed from the earth before these events play out.

Behold I tell you a mystery; we will not all sleep (die) but we will be changed, in a moment, in the twinkling of an eye, at the last trumpet; for the trumpet will sound, and the dead will be raised imperishable and we will be changed. 1 Corinthians 15.51-52.

New American Standard Bible.

For this we say to you by the word of the Lord, that we who are alive and remain until the coming of the Lord, will not proceed those who have fallen asleep. For the Lord Himself will descend from heaven with a shout, with the voice of the archangel and with the trumpet of God, and the dead in Christ will rise first. Then we who are alive and remain will be caught up (raptured) together with them in the clouds to meet the Lord in the air, and so we shall always be with the Lord. Therefore comfort one another with these words. I Thessalonians 4. 15-18 NASB

Chapter 28

Eyes to the Sky

'He answered me and said, 'Measure carefully in your mind, and when you see that some of the predicted signs have occurred, then you will know that it is the very time that the Most High is about to visit the world that he has made. So when there shall appear in the world earthquakes, tumult of peoples, intrigues of nations, wavering of leaders, confusion of princes, then you will know that it was of these that the Most High spoke from the days that were of old, from the beginning. For just as with everything that has occurred in the world, the beginning is evident and the end manifest; so also are the times of the Most High: the beginnings are manifest in wonders and mighty works, and the end in penalties (effects) and in signs.'2 Esdras 1-6

The end time cashless system, as predicted in scripture is here now. Central Bank Digital Currencies, have been independently and successfully 'stressed tested' under projects Hamilton and Lithium to determine its merits to the US Government, who are introducing this new system over the next two years, as well as planning how organisations will make their financial transactions. If, as expected, the 'Digital Dollar' is programmed by the United States Government, it would have in its possession the ultimate obedience tool and would sound the 'Death Nell' for all card and cash transactions. Anyone not complying with government regulations or having the temerity to protest or go on strike will have their electronic 'Buck' suspended or switched off. A simple pen stroke has consigned the freedoms that millions have fought and died for against tyrants for millennia into history's wastepaper basket. This system is about to be introduced **worldwide!**

In the days of St. Paul there were a noble group of people called the Bereans, Acts 17:11 who did not reject his teaching, instead they searched the scriptures to see if what he preached had merit. You owe it to yourself and your family to check the references and patents and do your own investigation. Ask God to reveal the truth about chemtrails. Observe how the aeroplane trails change over the course of fifteen minutes. Refuse to be side tracked by so-called 'fact checkers' who defend and are funded by powerful interest groups. Ask yourself why the United States has built over 800 FEMA camps that currently lay empty. What series of events are they expecting? Why would the US need such a comprehensive network of Deep Underground Military Bunkers or infrared satellites tracking NEO's if nothing is about to take place? The successfully launched James Web telescope works on a far deeper infrared spectrum than the Hubble telescope and can now make far more observations on what's approaching earth.

In the medical field, why are alternative treatments for coronavirus being ignored even though they have been successfully used as an early treatment for decades, and why are medical professionals who promote them being debunked and de-platformed? For what purpose has graphene oxide and luciferase been placed in the vaccines that have absolutely no medicinal benefits? The cashless system is now just a few years away as Morrison's, Sainsbury's, Tesco's and Lidl's are planning to introduce an Electronic Fund Transfer System that works off your fingerprint or facial recognition. You will shortly be unable to use your card or cash for any transactions.

To ensure that everyone complies with the NWO's draconian changes, the World Economic Forum has already begun it's

Orwellian brainwashing campaign with posters recently appearing showing a hapless smiling youth under which the wording states 'You will own nothing and be happy'. What they fail to say is that everything we have worked hard for over the years will be transferred over to *them*, for safe–keeping of course! The World Government will then loan us back what we already had but under a new 'lend lease' scheme, which will make them even happier! Au revoir property rights, Bonjour Gulag 'Resettlement Centres.' Guten Tag, FEMA Camps, Do Widzenia civil liberties! It is the knowledge of the approaching 'planetary doom' scenario that has dramatically accelerated us towards levels of government social control using Artificial Intelligence that even George Orwell would have found hard to contemplate.

There are two stark futures facing humanity: The New World Order's joyless draconian cashless society, akin to Communist China where we are all controlled, numbered and micro-chipped. A 'Hunger Games' world where food is in constant short supply. A place where we are followed everywhere by spy cameras linked to 5G networks and sent to 're-education' camps for the slightest infringement. Or, Christ's eternal plan for the redemption, restoration and renovation of the earth and establishment of *His* 1000 year Millennial Kingdom. It will be a time to heal and reverse the effects of a ruined earth after the devastating effects of the 7 year Antichrist's rule. Justice will at last prevail and everyone will feel safe and valued. This will be after a series of catastrophic end time events that nearly wipes out the world's population that the Bible calls 'The Great Tribulation'.

The FEMA Internment Camps are already set up. The underground tunnelling equipment that created the Deep Underground Military Bases is now silent. The millions of black plastic coffins ordered by the US Government's Centre for

Disease Control and Prevention are being kept in leased areas in farms across America.[178] The UK's mega prison complexes are ready. The new financial system is nearly in place.

A New Pandemic?

In October 2022 a new table-top exercise took place that closely resembled 'Event 201' mentioned earlier in this book. It followed the same themes including fictional news bulletins about lockdowns and travel restrictions. The exercise followed a supposed break-out of another pandemic in Brazil in 2025 called the 'Catastrophic Contagion or The Severe Epidemic Enterovirus Respiratory Syndrome.' A number of people from the African sub continent took part in the exercise, reporting how the virus was impacting their people. What is also of great concern are that nations within the United Nations are currently signing agreements with The World Health Organisation, which will allow them complete unfettered access to any country that suffers from any future pandemic. This will become a de-facto dictatorship controlled by an unelected body leading to an establishment of a Global Plutocracy.

Luke 21:28 'When these things begin to take place, stand up. Hold your head up with joy and hope. The time when you will be set free will be very close.' NIRC - New International Readers Version

Post Script

As the Jews were herded towards the concentration camps and the metal gates swung open, they noticed above each gate was written a short German phrase or saying. In Auschwitz it was 'Albert Mach Frie' which means 'Work Makes You Free.' This provided false hope that if the Jews worked hard enough they may one day be released. At Berkenwald Concentration Camp an old German proverb 'Jedem Das Seine' was quoted which roughly translated says, 'Everyone gets what they deserve'.

Is it true that everyone gets what they deserve? Did the Nazi scientists who were found guilty of crimes against humanity at Nuremburg but were then pardoned and shipped off to America to live a prosperous life, get what they deserved? Did the Jews get what they deserved when at the trial of Christ they placed a generational curse on themselves as they cried out 'Let his blood be on us and our children!' Matthew 27:25 Did Jesus, himself, get what he deserved when God, his heavenly Father, placed my sin and yours upon him as he died on the cross, so that the penalty of our sins would be covered? Now when we ask Christ's forgiveness, we can become born again by his Holy Spirit. The spotless Lamb of God died in your place and mine so that instead of going to Hell, we can gain entrance to Heaven through his blood. Satan was outwitted at the cross, for if he had known the plan of God for humanity, he would have never roused the crowd to kill the King of Glory. 1 Corinthians 2:8

There is a story of a father who needed to complete some paperwork at home, so to distract his daughter for a while, he gave her a jigsaw of the world and asked her to put it together for him. In what seemed just a few minutes the daughter ran excitedly into his study saying that she had already completed it. Thinking this was almost impossible he went and checked her work and was astonished to find that each piece had been properly fitted together. When the amazed father asked her how she had finished it so quickly, his daughter said 'Well Daddy, I saw that on the other side of the jigsaw there was a picture of Jesus and when I finished *that* picture the whole world just came together'.

Today we are living in a world that has abandoned its Christ-centred world view with people desperately trying to add things to their lives that were simply not made to fit. It is a desire for everything that leads to a feeling of emptiness.

The philosopher Pascal wrote 'There is a God shaped vacuum in the heart of every man which cannot be satisfied by any created thing but only by God the Creator made known through Jesus Christ'.

If you do not know Christ as your personal Saviour, then it's time to make the change. Although it is imperative to try to protect yourself and your family from the approaching storm, the only way to fully prepare is to ensure that you are living in a right relationship with God's son, Jesus Christ. Christianity is not just one of many different religious expressions; it allows repentant people to restore their broken relationship with their Creator. The Bible tells us that we must be 'born again' by God's Holy Spirit to become citizens of Heaven. John 3:7

If you are ready, say this simple prayer:

Dear Lord, I come to you in humility. I am fed up trying to live life my own way. I now choose to turn away from my sins and ask you to come into my life. I believe that when Jesus Christ died on the cross, he was dying in my place as he took my own personal sins with him onto the cross so that I could go free. Thank you for your love and forgiveness. I now ask for your Holy Spirit to enter my life and give me a new purpose and direction. I am now born again through the power of God and am committed to joining a Bible believing church and promise to get a full immersion baptism. AMEN!

Signed...Date...

References and Notes

Chapter One

The Nazis in America – A Warning from History

1. www.asomf.org/the-history-of-the-monument-men
2. www.worldwarfacts.org/joint-intelligence-objectives-agency
3. www.history.com/news/what-was-operation-paperclip
4. Operation Paperclip. The secret intelligence programme that brought Nazi scientists to America. Annie Jacobsen.
5. Ibid
6. Ibid
7. Ibid
8. Blind Eye To Murder. Tom Bower.
9. https://en.everybodywiki.com.com/MariaOrsic
10. Ibid
11. 63 Documents the Government Doesn't Want You to Read. Jesse Ventura.
12. Ibid
13. US Policy During WW 2 The CIA and Nazi War Criminals – Jewish Virtual Library

Chapter Two

Simon Wiesenthal Nazi Hunter

14. Murderers Amongst Us – Simon Wiesenthal
15. Ibid
16. Ibid
17. Ibid
18. Ibid

Chapter 3

America's and Germany's Eugenics Programme

19. https://antropology365.com/2017/08/24profiles-in-scientific-racism
20. The Ugly Truth Behind A Connecticut Survey That Reads like Nazi Propaganda
21. Buck v Bell https://www.americanherritage.com/race-cleansing-america
22. Ibid
23. Ibid
24. Ibid
25. The Horrifying American Roots of Nazi Eugenics Edwin Black
26. Ibid
27. Chemtrails Confirmed William Thomas
28. https://en.m.wikipedia.org/wiki/nazi-eugenics

Chapter 4

Obedience to Tyranny and Social Control

29. https://psychology.fas.harvard.edu/people/stanley-milgram
30. Ibid
31. Obedience to Authority Stanley Milgram
32. Ibid
33. Ibid
34. Ibid

Chapter 5

VaccineTyranny

35. Detection of Graphene in Covid 19 vaccinations by Micro-Ramen Spectroscopy Dr Campra Associate University Professor.

Almeria Spain Technical Report 02/11/2021.FINAL-VERSION-CAMPRA-REPORT-DETECTION-GRAPHENE—IN-COVID19-VACCINES.

36. Scanning & Transmission Electron Microscopy reveals Graphene Oxide in Cov19 Vaccines / Dr Robert Young.

37. What If- You were injected with Graphene Oxide – The What If Show.

38. Validity Of Key Studies On Origin Of Coronavirus In Doubt Science Journals Investigating. US Right To Know. November9,2020. https://www.organicconsumers.org

39. www.healthline.com/health/cold-flu/flu shot ingredients

40. Commission Removes Legal Aid For Parents Suing Over MMR Vaccine. https://www.Dmj.com

41. www.bbc.com/news/uk/uk-52219070

42. www.mencap.org.uk/press-release/eight-10deaths-people-learning-disability-are-covid-related-inequality-soars

43. National Sciences Advisory Board. https://www.nih.gov/about-nih/who-we-are/nih-directorstatements/statement-usabbs-march-30-2022

Chapter 6

Gain of Function Research

44. United States Institute for Health December-9-2017 https://www.nih.gov/about-nih/who-we-are/nihdirector/statements/nih-funding-pause-gain-ffunctionresearch/

45. Midazolam can depress breathing https://www.drugs.com/stx/midazolam-side-effects

46. https://evidencenotfear.com/tag/professorpatrickPullicino

47. https://www.theguardian.com/society/2020/december/03/do-not-resuscitate-orders-caused-potentially-avoidable-deaths

48. Maraks Disease – a Cautionary Tale? https://notesfromthesocialclinic.org

49. 1918 Flu Antibodies Resurrected From Elderly Survivors August 18th 2008https://www.ons.gov.uk/aboutus/trans parencyandgovernancefreedomofinformationfoi/deathscaused bycovid19only
50. Un-blinding Placebo-Controlled Covid-19 Vaccine Trials. A.M.A. Journal of Ethics
51. The 10 Biggest Pfizer Company Lawsuits in Company History lawyerinc.com/biggest-pfizer-lawsuits/

Chapter 7

The Origins Of Evil

Notes All Biblical references appear within this Chapter. The Book of Enoch is not considered a 'biblical book' and is not contained within the Cannon of Scripture. However it provides insight into the fall of the Angels that are only touched on briefly in Genesis 6. This is the only particular manuscript that is addressed to the last Generation of believers just before the return of Christ. The way parts of it were unearthed in Quram in 1947 at the same time Israel was becoming a re-born nation cannot be just a coincidence.

Notes The book of Jasher is not part of the Old Testament and should be treated as a historical document. It provides a backdrop to ancient biblical events and adds additional information on these times. It is referenced in Joshua 10 vs 13, 2 Samuel 1 vs 18 and 2 Timothy 3 vs 8.

Chapter 8

God's judgement on the Fallen Angels

All biblical, apocryphal and other references are included in this chapter

Chapter 9

Nimrod, the Tower of Babel and the First Global Government

All biblical apocryphal and other references are included in this chapter

Chapter 10

The New World Order and the World's Second Global Governance

52. The Constantinople Letter of 1489 www.pateo.nt/HTML/EN/pateopedia/subjects/constantinope_letter.htm
53. World-Wide Evil and Misery. The Legacy Of The 13 Satanic Bloodlines. Robin De Ruiter and Fritz Springmeier
54. Ibid
55. AdamWeishaupt Biography https://www.thefamouspeople.com/profiles/adam-weishaupt
56. Who Controls All of Our Money? Coldfusion YouTube video
57. Note- Executive Order 11110 Signed by John F Kennedy on June 4th 1963 gave the U.S. the right to circulate its own money and dollar bills begun to be printed with 'United States Note' rather than Federal Reserve Note. The bills were backed up with 4.292 billion dollars of silver giving the money an intrinsic value which would be used without having to pay interest to the Federal Reserve. Some notes started to circulate just before Kennedy was murdered, after which they were hurriedly withdrawn from circulation. After the Bay of Pigs disaster where the Military Industrial Complex had tried to trick Kennedy into entering a phony war. Kennedy fired CIA Director Allen Dulles and is reported to have said to have vowed to 'splinter the CIA into, a thousand pieces and scatter it into the winds.'https://www.fff.org2021/05/13

58. en.wikipedia.org/wiki/mediaconglomerate

59. Worldwide Evil and Misery- The legacy of the 13 Satanic Bloodlines -Robin de Ruiter& Fritz Springmeier

60. https://therealuncensoredthruthrobgrant.substack.com/p/bilderberg-group

61. https://economiccollapssenews.com Liz Truss https://mises.org/wiki/no-privacey-no-property-world-2030-according-wef Author's note: Born in 1938 Klaus Schwab is a son of Eugen Wilhelm Schwab. His father was the head of the ESCHER WYSS Engineering Company that made flame throwers and other industrial parts for the Nazi war effort. They were declared a special Nazi model company and received an award for this work. The company was also involved in the distillation of heavy water for the enrichment of uranium which would be used for nuclear bombs. The company used slave labour from Ravensburg and over 600 workers were euthanized.

62. www.cmhi.com.hk/why-china-is-buying-up-us-farms

63. Klaus Schwab states that the W.E.F. has infiltrated governments around the world. You Tube Video Amy Adams 20/02/2022.

64. Trudeau and Rutte 'golden pin-up boys' for world economic forum; Rowan Dean 06/07/2022 Sky News Australia

65. www.operationreachthelost.com/worshiping-molech-child-sacrifice-bohemiangrove

66. ibid

67. https://historyheist.com/the-club-of-rome-issues-a-report-entitled-regionized-and-adaptive-model-of-the-global-world

68. blogspot.com/2011/11un-divides-the-world-into-10-regional.html

69. qz.com/the-who-is-too-dependent-on-gates-foundation-donations

Chapter 11

CERN's Hadron Collider and the Bottomless Pit

70 https://www.christianevidence.net/201/05/cern-and-bible-prophecy.html.

71. https://www.fritjofcapra.net/shivas-cosmic-dance-at-cern/

72. Inside the World's Largest Science Experiment- Physics Girl Why this stuff costs $2700 trillion per gram-antimatter at CERN.

73. Finding 'God' particle could destroy the universe warns Stephen Hawking https://www.dailymail.co.uk/news/article-2746727

74. Symmetry-CERN dance-opera film (official trailer) 1st February 2016.

75. https://www.express.co.uk/news/science/1323952/Black-hole-could-be-created-on-earth-after-Einstein-general-relativity-challenged.

76. https://www.undertorah.com/pdf/a-dangerous-situation-arising-part-3pdf

77. Large Hadron Collider switches on at highest ever power level to look for dark matter. https://www.livescience.com Ben Turner arcticle 25/07/2022

Chapter 12

Changes Taking Place to the Authorised King James Bible

All Biblical references appear within this chapter

Chapter 13

Type and Antitype – History Repeating Itself

78. https;//wwwliquisearch.com/gaius-popillius-launus

79. https;// gotquestions.org/Antiochus-Epiphanies.html
80. Ibid
81. Ibid

Chapter 14

The Transhuman Agenda

82. https://www.newscientist.com/definition/what-is-crispr
83. https::://www.newscientist.com/question/what-is-a-chimera
84. Trans-evolution The coming Age Of Human Deconstruction – David Estulin

Chapter 15

The Dark History Of Bill Gates

85. www.industrytap.com/knowledge-doubling-every-12-months-soon-to-be-every-12-hours/3950
86. https://trisentennial.us/2020/03/28/bill-gates-father-ran-planned-parenthood-his-mother-created-microsoft-together-they-trained-their-son-to-spread-the-gospel-of-eugenics/eug?ft
87. 80% of Planned Parent Offices are in surgical abortion facilities in minority communities. Founder of Planned Parenthood had ties to white Supremacy and Eugenics. EWTN News Nightly April 20th 2021.
88. Women and the New Race Margaret Sanger
89. Margaret Sangers Multifaceted Defence of Abortion and Infanticide. Anne Barbeau Gardiner https://www.uffl.org/vol16/gardiner06.pdf
90. Margaret Sanger wanted to exterminate Negros. Clarence J Gamble letter December 10th 1939. Liberty Under Attack September 22nd 2015 &Smith Libraries.org

91. Objectivism The Ayn Rand Society- Objectivism is a concept of man being a 'heroic being' with his own happiness as the moral purpose of his life, with productive achievement as his noblest activity and reason as his only absolute.
92. https://www.jewishvirtuallibray.org/alangreenspan
93. https://expose-news.com/2021/07/24/bill-gate-funds-mhra-and-shares-in-pfizer/
94. Ibid
95. https://www.dailymail.co.uk/news/article-2908963/judges-demand-answers-children-die-controversial-cancer-vaccine-trial-india
96. https://informedchoicewa.org/education/bill-gates--and-intellectual-ventures-fund-microchip-implant-vaccine-technology/
97. https;//grandmageri422.me/2021/02/07/bill-gates-madam-blavatski-alice-bailey-the-lucis-trust-and-the-occult
98. http://wwwcentreforhealthsecurity.org

Chapter 16

Countdown to Catastrophe

99. https://humanoriginproject.com-two-suns-binary-star-model
100. https://www.rawgist.com/chilean-astronomer-carlos-munoz-ferrada-predictshercobulusakaplanet-x/
101. https://solarstory.net/planets/planet-x
102. Interview to Dr. Robert S Harrington by ZachariaSitcthin February 28th 2008 https://.news.sbs.com-au-worldnewsaustralia
103. Sounds on the Golden Record - https://voyager-jpl.nasa.gov
104. https://www.jpl.nasa.gov/missions/infrared-astronomical-satellite-iras

105. https://astrobiology.nasa.gov/news/caltech-researchers-find-evidence-of-a-real-ninth-planet/

106. Note-The OORT Cloud named after Jan OORT who discovered it is a large field of rocks and comets that extends far beyond our solar system. The Kuiper belt surrounds our solar system in closer proximity and contains a vast array of icy particles, dust and debris.

Chapter 17

Evidence that the Earth is being affected by an External Force

107. A doubling of the suns coronal magnetic field over the past 100 years - Mike Lockwood et al. Nature vol 399 3/06/1999 www.Nature.com

108. Something is Affecting our entire Solar System –nemesis maturity posted 24/06/2015

109. Sun Blamed For Warming Of Earth and Other Worlds. https://www.livescience.com/1349-sun-blamed-warming-earth-worlds.html 12/03/2007

110. Study projects a surge in coastal flooding starting in 2030. https://www.nasa.gov

111. Earths Magnetic Field Is Acting Up And Geologists Don't Know Why. https://www.nature.com/articles/041585-019-00007-1/ 09/01/2019

112. Greenland's Ice Sheet Is melting but much of the heating is coming from INSIDE the earth. https://www.dailymail.00.015spacetech

113. What Will Happen When Earths North And South Poles Flip? Tech Insider Posted 05/04/2018

114. Fish Navigation Mystery Solved As Trout Study Finds Magnetic Cells That Point The Way. https://www.huffpost.com

115. Coast to Coast Interview between Art Bell and Malachi Martin. April 5th 1997

116. Sink Holes detection in a residential area in the State of Kuwait – Arabian Journal for Science and Engineering. Hasan Kamal Et al.

117. https://www.cbsnews.com/news/a-giant-crack-opens-in-Kenya-but-what's/causing/it/

118. Massive Sink Holes leave two missing and three injured in Guatamala. https://www.abs.net.au/news/2022-09-26

119. https://truthinplainsight.com/fema-concentration-camp-location-list/wayside December 20th 2020

120. https://theeventchronicle.com/list-of-deep-underground-basis/JohnMorse 29th November 2016

121. https://www.mitchellson.co.uk/projects/glen-parva-prison-leicester/s17081/

122. https://www.bbc.co.uk/news/uk-england-northamptonshire-54436827

123. https;//www.spaceforce.mil/about-us/Fact-sheets/

124. https://science.nasa.gov/nasa-hubble-spots-twin-tails-in-new-image-after-dart-impact

125. National Near-Earth Object Preparedness Strategy And Action Plan - Published 2018

126. Robert Harrington interview with Zachariah Sitchen - posted 22/09/12 - Planet 7 X

127. https://themilleniumreport.com2015/01/chillean-astronomer-carlos-munoz-Ferrada-predicts-hercolobus-aka-planet-x/

128. Ibid

129. Internet Archive -Television interview with Munoz Ferrada on Misterios Y Enigma's Spanish Channel 4 programme.

130. GEO-ENGINERING RESEARCH –Parliamentary Office of Science and Technology Postnote- March 2009 Number 327.

Chapter 18

The IPCC and the Medieval Warm Period

131. http://scienceandpublicpolicy.org/images/stories/papers/originals/climate_money.
132. https://sites.google.com/sites/medievalwarmperiod/Home
133. Hull Doomsday Project 45. Doomsday Book 1087 Vineyards Providing Top Quality Wine https://www.doomsdaybook.net
134. http://www.pbs.org/wgbh/pages/frontline/hotpolitics/interviews/wirth.html
135. https://www.forbes.com/sites/jamestaylor/2011/11/23/climate-2-0-climate-new-e-mails-rock-the-global-warming-debate/
136. https://thenewamerican.com/noaa-and-weather-station-numbers-were-dramatically-cut-the-new-climategate-scandal/
137. www.americanthinker.com/articles/2010/02/climatgates-phil-jomes-confes.hmtl.
138. https://www.dailymail.co.uk/news/article1235395/SPECIAL-INVESTIGATION-climate-change-emails-row-deepens-russians-admit-they-DID-come-from-their-siberian-server
139. Keeling Curve https://education.nationalgeographic.org/resource/keeling-curve

Chapter 19

The Pope, The Vatican's Infrared Telescope and the Secretum Omega.

140. https://en.wikipedia.org/wiki/Vatican-Advanced-Technology-Telescope
141. The Max Planck Institute for Extraterrestrial Physics – LUCI A Near-Infrared Camera and Spectograph for the

Large Binocular Telescope https://www.mpe.mpg.de/ir//lucifer.

142. Secretum Omega- Interview with the Jesuit Christiaforo Berbato.

After repeated efforts to contact Christiaforo to ask permission to use this article – I discovered that he had applied for and been granted, under European Law, The right to be forgotton'. This is also known as 'The Right To Erasure 'under article 17 of the General Data Protection Regulation. Any E.U. citizen can request to have all electronic records relating to their online presence, removed. This article now only exists from other websites that have copied it.

142. Ibid

143. Ibid

144. Ibid

146. The Birth of Tammuz and Polytheism – The Fuel Project.

147. Roman Catholic Beliefs - https://romancatholicbeliefs.org/the-popes-cardinals-bishops-and-priests-or-rome-are-worshippers-of-the-sun-god-tummuz

148. https://www.bibliotecapleyedes.net/ciencia/ciencia-brain 65.hmtl

Chapter 20

Obedience Tools Of The New World Order- 1 Weather Warfare

149. https://themilleniumreport.com/2018/11/indigo-skyfold-u-s-air-force-pilot-exposes-top-secret-chemtrail-plogram-an-ongoing-deep-state-operation/ November 25/2018

152. Ibid

153. Chemtails Confirmed - William Thomas Bridger House Publications

154. Ibid

155. Ibid

156. www.stopsprayingcalifornia.com/morgellons-disease-&-chemtrails.php.

Chapter 21

Obedience Tools of the New World Order 2 – Space, Psychotronic and Financial Control Systems.

157. The New World Order Book – Nick Redfern Visible Ink Press
158. Ibid
159. https://wikipedia.org/wiki/Denver-International-Airport
160. https://allthatsinteresting.com/denver-airport-conspiracy.
161. https://wikipedia.org/wiki/Denver-International-Airport
162. https://en.wikipedia.org/wiki/Patriot-Act
163. Ibid
164. https://carnicominstitute.com/space-preservation-act-of-2001-introduced-in-the-house-horourable-rep-Kucinich/
165. HAARP – The Ultimate Weapon Of The Conspiracy Terry E Smith
166. https://stocktrendalernts.com/what-are-biden-bucks-jim-rickards-latest-prediction/
167. Ibid
168. https://www.upward.news/ftx-scandle-explained/

Chapter 22

Between a rock and a Hard Place

169. https://solarsystem.nasa.gov/asteroids-comets-and-meteors/asteroids/apophis-in-depth
170. https://skywatchtv.com/2021/03/30/impact/
171. https://spaceguardcentre.com/the-space-guard/

Note - The underfunded UK Space-guard Centre is located in Knighton Powys

172. https;//www.stastica.com/chart/17453/space-collision-asteroid/

Chapter 23

Biblical Patterns and Parallels

173. rediscovering.thebookofenoch.info
174. https://deadsea.com/explore/historical-sites/biblical-sites/the-dead-sea-scrolls/

Chapter 24

Down the Rabbit Hole

175. https://www.sparknotes.com/lit/1984/summary/
176. https://www.sparknotes.com/lit/bravenew/
177. https://en.wikipedia.org/wiki/the-prisoner

Chapter 25

The last 2 churches

All references are contained within the chapter

Chapter 26

Satan's Busted Flush

All references are contained within this chapter

Chapter 27

Pre Rapture and Tribulation Prophecies

All references are contained within this chapter

Chapter 28

Eyes to the Sky

All references are contained within this chapter

Post Script

178. Fema Camp Coffins Investigated Boomya 555 You Tube video

Also by this Author

Peter's Progress An updated retelling of Pilgrims Progress for young people that includes illustrations. Peter, Fish, Cobra and Penny head off to find the 'Stairway to Heaven' making friends while fending off the forces of darkness.

APOCALYPSE NOW - The Final Countdown A book of eclectic and revealing poetry with a focus on the end times Both are available from Lulu publications www.lulu.com

Milton Keynes UK
Ingram Content Group UK Ltd.
UKHW050901150923
428733UK00011B/120